Constantine
on Peopleware

Constantine on Peopleware

Larry L. Constantine

Professor of Computing Sciences
University of Technology, Sydney

Principal Consultant
Constantine & Lockwood, Ltd.

YOURDON PRESS
Prentice Hall Building
Englewood Cliffs, New Jersey 07632

Library of Congress Cataloging-in Publication Data

Constantine, Larry L.
    Constantine on Peopleware / Larry Constantine.
        p.   cm. (Yourdon Press computing series)
    Includes bibliographical references
    ISBN 0-13-331976-8
    1. Computer software--Development.   I. Title.
QA76.76.D47C655   1995
005. 1--dc20
                                                94-41384
                                                    CIP

Editorial/production supervision
    and interior design: *Harriet Tellem*
Cover design: *DEFRANCO Design, Inc.*
Manufacturing manager: *Alexis Heydt*
Acquisitions editor: *Paul W. Becker*
Editorial assistant: *Maureen Diana*
Cover illustration credit: *Phil Huling / The Stock Illustration Source, Inc.*

Published by Prentice Hall P T R
Prentice-Hall, Inc.
A Simon & Schuster Company
Englewood Cliffs, New Jersey 07632

The publisher offers discounts on this book in bulk quantities.
For more information contact:

            Corporate Sales Department
            Prentice Hall P T R
            113 Sylvan Avenue
            Englewood Cliffs, New Jersey 07632

            Phone: 201-592-2498, 800-382-3419
            FAX: 201-592-2249, e-mail: dan_rush@prenhall.com

Printed in the United States of America
    10   9   8   7   6   5   4   3   2   1

ISBN 0-13-331976-8

Prentice-Hall International (UK) Limited, *London*
Prentice-Hall of Australia Pty. Limited, *Sydney*
Prentice-Hall Canada Inc., *Toronto*
Prentice-Hall Hispanoamericana, S.A., *Mexico*
Prentice-Hall of India Private Limited, *New Delhi*
Prentice-Hall of Japan, Inc., *Tokyo*
Simon & Schuster Asia Pte. Ltd., *Singapore*
Editora Prentice-Hall do Brasil, Ltda., *Rio de Janeiro*

Dedication

*To LADL, who finally taught me
the meaning of partnership.*

Contents

Foreword by
Meilir Page-Jones

"Peopleware?" he thundered as I slunk from his office. PEOPLEWARE?

It was the heyday of computer-aided software engineering and I had been hired as a consultant to choose the best CASE tool to solve the problems of a large corporate shop. I prowled around, studied their systems, and interviewed their programmers and analysts. As I did so, I began to realize that a CASE tool would be about as useful to them as a surfboard to a Gobi nomad. They needed a better work environment, more supportive management, a greater team spirit, and more training in software methods. The last thing that they needed was another tool.

In my report to management I pointed out that an investment in some new technological solution, though tempting and easy to make, was irrelevant to their immediate needs. Until the shop invested more in its human assets, any investment in another whiz-bang tool would be wasted. Rather than in hardware and software, management should be investing in *peopleware*, I suggested.

It was then, of course, that I was thrown out of this manager's office. Behind me, at his large gizmo-encrusted desk, I left a superb specimen of *Homo Machinarum*. He just hadn't understood. But he did have an excuse: He'd never had the opportunity to read *Constantine on Peopleware*.

Last year I visited a project that was tap-dancing in quicksand. Whenever anyone produced anything, the result was argument, confusion, and lowered morale. All the team members were bright and motivated, but their angst and frustration was palpable. After less than a morning I realized what was wrong.

The project was, on one level, a traditional, corporate-application, development project. (The application was inventory management.) However, it had a non-traditional twist — a second team had been chartered to investigate hand-held bar coders and portable computers mounted on forklift trucks. Ironically, the main team was organized as a breakthrough team and the second team was organized as a rigid tactical pyramid.

The two teams' styles derived from the personalities of their respective leaders. My first recommendation was simply that the teams switch leaders. When this switch paid dividends they were all impressed. But I didn't give away my secret: I'd read Constantine's columns on Peopleware and they hadn't.

Early this year I was called in for the final review of a shop's first attempts at GUIs (graphical user interfaces). What I saw was subtly shocking. In one window, the most frequent user response required three mouse clicks — in the NE, NW, and SE corners of the window. Another (similar) window required clicks in the SW and NW corners, followed by a double-click in the SE corner. On some windows, command buttons were laid along the bottom, starting on the left; on other windows, they were laid along the bottom, starting on the right; on other windows they were laid out vertically; and on some windows buttons were gigantic, taking up much of the window.

To get the full picture, add in a few not-so-subtle features: windows with eight clashing colors that could have won "Gaudiness of the Year" awards, SAVE commands sometimes under FILE and sometimes under EDIT, and command buttons that acquired purple racing stripes when they were pressed. When I asked the project team what on earth the users thought of all this chaos and inconsistency, I received blank stares. No one had thought to consult the users on their system interface.

My advice that the team scrap the entire interface, develop standards, and work with the users to capture their best ways of working was coldly rejected. So was my attempt at humor. (How about a message stating: "SOME WINDOWS CONTAIN SCENES OF GRAPHIC VIOLENCE?") My final piece of advice — read Constantine's column on Peopleware — was also ignored. But six months later, after the users had tossed out the entire system, I got a call from the project's new leader: "What was that reference on Peopleware again?"

That's an easy one: It's the book in your hands now. Go ahead, leap into it. I learned so much from this book about people working with computer systems, people working on developing computer systems, and people working with people. I also discovered things that I already knew — but didn't know that I knew.

Even if you work alone, or develop systems that no one uses, or disagree with everything that Larry says, this book may still enchant you. His writing is (like Larry himself) graceful, erudite, witty, and charming. As I reviewed the book for this foreword, I found that I couldn't put it down. (And I've already read it twice before!)

Larry has a knack for presenting apparently familiar material from an unfamiliar perspective. Perhaps this is because Larry is both an insider to our field and an outsider. As early as the 1960s he was researching and writing his classic work on structured systems design. But he is also as comfortable in the study of human interactions as he is in software.

He illuminates and warms every subject he examines. The light that he shines into software development has allowed several people I know to sparkle. Including me.

Enjoy!

Meilir Page-Jones
Bellevue, WA

Foreword by Bill Curtis

The circle has been closed!

In the first epoch only the hardware mattered. Hardware was expensive. Software was cheap, and so were the people who developed it. Only the elite used computers, and they could master the most arcane of interfaces. Programmers learned to write programs from wizards. Programs were called 'beautiful' because they used the hardware artfully, not because most people could use them.

In the second epoch hardware became cheaper and software grew far larger and more expensive. Swarms of programmers began emerging from the universities. The growing uses for computers required an avalanche of software. Software development became a team activity. People were told to manage what had a few years before been considered an art. Programmers learned to write programs using a method developed by someone named Constantine. Then he dropped out of sight and programmers had to learn from someone else. Programs were called 'beautiful' because other programmers could understand them, not because most people could use them.

The third epoch started with Jerry Weinberg's The Psychology of Programming in 1971. Hardware eventually became a commodity and everyone started buying personal computers. Having bought computers, they had to figure out how to use them. Common folk had crashed the ball, but thanks to the complexity of the steps, they couldn't join the dance. The first mavens of usability design used social science terms like 'software psychology' and programmers paid little attention. But then from exile returns Constantine, this time to legitimize discussion of human issues among the software elite. Programs will now be called 'beautiful' because their functionality and interface are usable, and most people will use them.

Raising human issues in a domain dominated by engineers and computer scientists has been contrarian, and those who did it were usually accorded little respect. Yet when one of the earliest contributors to the discipline begins discussing human issues, software engineers can join the dialogue without fear of losing stature. In the first and second epochs, the art and discipline of programming lay somewhere other than in the user interface.

In the 1970s it was only the 'soft' fringe of software engineering that worried about human issues in computing. The first conference on Human Factors in Computing Systems convened in Gaithersburg, Maryland in March 1982. Instead of the projected 200, 907 people attended the first in the very successful CHI conference series. A profession specializing in human-computer interaction emerged during the 1980s. These specialists focused on areas such as the usability of human interfaces, the psychology of programming, and the technology to support cooperative activities. In the mid-1980s Apple Computer proved with the Macintosh that usability could be a market issue. By the end of the 1980s most large software development organizations had started building usability labs.

In the mid-1980s Tom DeMarco and Tim Lister were resensitizing software developers to the dramatic impact people issues could have on development performance in their book, *Peopleware*. Having spent his years out of software in the world of family therapy, Larry Constantine returned to software engineering with new insights into how people issues should be handled in software development. These insights are crucial to anyone wanting to increase their software development performance.

This book is important not just because it delves into the human issues in software development — such books have been written before by specialists writing for other specialists. This book is important because it was written for practicing software engineers by one of their own. In his first software career Larry Constantine made original contributions on how computer programs should be designed to ease the burden of other programmers who interact with them. In his second career Larry Constantine is making original contributions on how computer programs should be designed to ease the burden of anyone who interacts with them. The circle is closed now that one of the icons of software engineering has come to focus squarely on the human issues in computing.

Bill Curtis
In the hills above Austin

Acknowledgments

This book has been a group effort from the get-go. There would be no book had there not been a column from which to compile its contents. There would have been no column without Larry O'Brien at Miller Freeman Publications. He offered me the prime real estate in his magazine to write about whatever truly interested me. Larry has been a great editor, abetted by a succession of other talented people at *Computer Language Magazine* and *Software Development*, including Gretchen Bay, Nicole Freeman, Michele Gahee, and Nicole Claro; all of whom have had to cope with my syntax and my stupid e-mail. I also want to thank other friends and editors — Tony Nash and Ed Yourdon at *American Programmer*, and Marie Lenzie at *Object Magazine* — for providing a forum for viewpoints a standard deviation or two off the norm.

To ever patient, ever flexible, Paul Becker, my editor at Prentice Hall; my thanks for switching courses to bring this book to print. To Harriet Tellem, Senior Production Editor; my gratitude for saving me from my own misplaced faith that the manuscript was already flawless. To the list of editors who have improved my work, I must also add my favorite, Lucy Lockwood; who knows when my writing sings and when it sinks as well as how to convince me of the difference. Thanks Lucy. Thanks all.

Introduction

Hardware, Software, Peopleware

Good software does not come from CASE tools, visual programming, rapid prototyping, or object technology. Good software comes from people. So does bad software. In 1992, I started writing a regular column with this simple premise: since software is created by people and used by people, a better understanding of people — how they work, how they do their work, and how they work together — is a basis for better software development and better software. The subject of the column was not hardware, not software, but peopleware.

In a field peppered with neologisms, peopleware is one of those few that really needed to be invented. Peter G. Newmann, perhaps best known for his regular reports on the human risks and real hazards of computers and computer programs, appears to have been the first to use the term in print, in a 1976 paper called "Peopleware in Systems" in an obscure book that took its title from the paper. The word seems to have been independently coined by Meilir Page-Jones, who used it in the 1980 edition of his *Practical Guide to Structured Systems Design,* the book that finally made my work on structured design understandable to the average programmer. But peopleware most likely became lodged in the permanent lexicon of our field with the 1987 publication of a great little book by that title from Tom DeMarco and Tim Lister. In calling my column "Peopleware," I was cribbing from the best.

Peopleware is really the third frontier of the computer revolution. First came the hardware crisis. At one time we thought our problems were really due to hardware. If only we had faster and more powerful computers, we thought, with more memory and better peripherals, then we could build better systems; we could solve our problems. Well, we got better computers. Year after year the hardware grew swifter, the memories larger, and the peripherals more versatile and ergonomic. And our problems persisted. We still delivered hard-to-use systems; we still ran late and over budget with our projects. So we concluded that the real problem was software, and the front lines in the revolution shifted to what many came to call "the software crisis." If only we had better tools, higher level languages, richer component libraries, and programs to help us build programs, then we could solve our problems and deliver good systems on time and within budget. The third-generation languages grew more sophisticated and begat 4GLs. Compilers grew faster and more clever. Libraries of reusable components expanded, editors became context-sensitive, and computer-aided software engineering tools sprang up from every point of the compass. On the heels of the structural revolution that gave us structured design and analysis, object orientation began to mature and gained in popularity. Still, schedules kept slipping and budgets kept busting, and everywhere the bugs remained stubbornly bugs.

At last, like Pogo and his fabled friends from Okeefenokee, we were forced to recognize where the problem lay. "We have met the enemy and they is us," said the unwittingly wise little possum. Indeed. Peopleware is the real issue. We are the problem and we are the solution. How convenient.

Peopleware spans a pretty broad panorama. Anything that has to do with the role of people in the software and applications development process is within the purview of peopleware. The column, like this book, touches on an assortment of issues scattered around that landscape: quality and productivity, teamwork, group dynamics, personality and programming, project management and organizational issues, interface design and human-machine interaction, cognition, psychology, and thought processes.

All of these things interest and excite me. They always have. I took my degree in management in part because it allowed me to mix computers and systems theory with psychology. My thesis was on the psychology of computer programming. I introduced psychologist George Miller and his magical number (7±2, of course) to thousands of students and dozens of colleagues over the years. The structure of structure charts was carefully devised to aid visual concept formation and problem solving. Coupling and cohesion, those venerable metrics at the heart of structured design, are really about computer programs as viewed by people. What makes programs complex or simple is precisely whatever is complex or simple to the minds of the programmers who write, maintain, and modify them.

In a sense, I can't stay away from the people issues any more than I can stay away from computers. I thought I had escaped when I bid farewell to the computer field in July of 1976, declaring my independence even as America celebrated the bicentennial of its independence. Trained as a family therapist, I ended up spending more than a decade in private and agency practice working with couples and families and troubled adolescents. But the forces of the universe conspired to steer me back toward the technological frontier.

Peopleware is a crossroads on that frontier, a junction where highways from my different worlds intersect. Management, organization development, personality, modeling, tools, methods, process, human-computer interaction, whatever. At one time or another I've written and worked and taught in all of these areas. The column has given me the excuse to wander again over the landscape, like a Charles Kuralt, stopping to explore interesting ideas, taking up challenges where they arose, cruising the interstates and county roads of software and applications development.

This book logs the journey so far, starting out in *Computer Language Magazine* and continuing in the retitled *Software Development*. The column is still just called "Peopleware." Here are the first thirty-something columns and a few closely related side trips published in other places. The essays and articles have been edited for continuity, and some material that was deleted when they were cut to length for magazine publication, has been restored. This, then, is the "director's cut," arranged into quasi-logical sections that contribute to a certain illusion of organization. But this is no encyclopedia or textbook, not even a road map of the vast territory of peopleware, just the journal of one pilgrim.

The pilgrimage continues.

1

Group Development

Introduction

Michelangelo, that paradigm of the lone genius, did not work alone. The Sistine Chapel was not the lonely labor of an isolated artist, but a group effort overseen and coordinated by Michelangelo. His genius, it turns out, was not for art alone, but for the art of managing a team. He called his artists and artisans by their first names or nicknames. He encouraged initiative, cooperation, and pride in workmanship. He would have been at home in a meeting on software quality management.

Software development is group development. Whether it's a matter of art or engineering, most software comes out of a collective enterprise in which a group of developers work together or at odds on a common system. How the group carries out its discussions, its decisions, and its digressions will have a lot to do with how good the work turns out. It is easier to build good software if you have a group that works well together, one that copes with conflict without collapse, one that uses its resources efficiently and effectively.

Group development also refers to the development *of* groups, to the processes and practices that can transform a mere assemblage into a high-performance team. Many programmers view group development and team building with a certain skepticism. They don't cotton to cheerleading or chants or group games that seem only to support a superficial team spirit. Such touchy-feely stuff is not for them. They were selected for their programming skills, not their social skills, for coding more than for cooperation.

Because understanding the language of groups and group processes may be every bit as important as understanding a programming language, this book starts with an exploration of how groups work and how they can work better to develop better software.

Decisions, Decisions *

There is more than one way. There is always more than one way. This simple credo has been a practical beacon throughout my professional life, leading me to consider alternatives in how software might be organized and how people might be organized. But recognizing alternatives also carries a burden, the burden of making decisions. Developing better software means making choices among alternatives and, better still, finding that creative synthesis that integrates the best of several approaches and thereby exceeds them all. Well-organized teams that base decision making and problem solving on consensus have the best shot at making quality decisions and building such a creative synthesis, but they need to know how to avoid certain traps common to groups. The secrets of consensus-based teamwork are worth exploring.

I have always considered the ability to make decisions to be one of the most essential of basic life skills. There is no way to learn how except by doing it which means that successful families and companies make sure there is plenty of opportunity to practice the real thing. By mid-career, the typical professional programmer has solved countless problems and along the way has probably made many thousands of decisions. Naturally, we expect professionals to become good at it. But most of these decisions will have been made individually, by the programmer on her or his own, and problem solving and decision making in groups are different animals altogether.

* From *Computer Language Magazine,* Volume 9, #3, March 1992.

Risks of Mediocrity

In the dark ages, when I was first learning about management and group dynamics at M.I.T.'s Sloan School, much study and concern were focused on supposed defects of group problem solving and decision making, particularly the effects of the so-called risky shift and the counter-tendency of groups to pull toward a mediocre mean. In those conservative days, even democratically minded managers worried more about the risky-shift than about creeping mediocrity. The upheavals of the 1970s lay ahead, and groupthink was the zeitgeist.

According to the research, collective decisions often seemed to be skewed toward more risky alternatives than would be selected by members deciding independently. If this model applied to programming, we would expect groups to produce software that used more exotic data structures or more unconventional algorithms or more obscure language features. However, other research on group dynamics seemed to show that groups had a leveling effect on problem solving and decision making that reduced results to a kind of lowest common denominator of individual contributions and abilities. Either way, the lone decision maker seemed to have an edge.

It turns out that both effects depend largely on the way a group is organized and led. In Russia, where I have worked with consultants and managers involved in new enterprises, the mediocre mean appears to have dominated the old Soviet-based system. To many of the managers trained under the old regimes, teamwork meant being dragged down to levels of common incompetency. In Soviet management, teams were often a way to avoid responsibility; sometimes they actively conspired to limit performance. To take a stand or advance a novel or controversial idea in such a team, indeed to stand out in any way, was not only to risk the resentment of peers but perhaps to be held accountable and then expected to repeat the performance on future efforts. With the ultimate job security of the typical Soviet sinecure and no rewards for practical performance, why bother?

The social and organizational climate in which a group works is what really shapes the ability to perform up to potential. For best results, the corporate culture and group leadership must actively encourage and support innovation and collaboration. In a sense, the Soviet teams did perform well, meeting the *real* expectations of bosses and enterprise policy makers, which were based more on covering the backside than achieving results. Soviet managers told me they all learned "never be the last link in a chain."

Leading Lightly

In consensus design and decision making, the role of the group leader is crucial, not only in establishing the overall climate for collaboration but also in the detailed way in which leadership is exercised. Consensus design and decision making is at its best when the solution derives from the talents of all team members and reflects the experience, creativity, and critical thinking of all, not just an average of their contributions, but a genuine synthesis that combines their best. When group leaders, however talented and brilliant, push their own agenda, the quality of teamwork goes down.

The effect of group leadership can be as insidious as it is subtle. Even just expressing an opinion at the wrong time can bias a group and lead to a poorer outcome. Research has shown that merely having leaders delay tossing in their own ideas until after all or most group members have presented theirs will improve the group solutions. That means that a leader who merely speaks too soon is probably degrading the quality of teamwork. Confident leaders, sure that they are right or know best, may cause the most difficulty.

Most project leaders and mid-level managers in software development are really techies at heart. Nearly every one of them was promoted up from programming, systems analysis, and software engineering. They got where they are by being good at software development. For many, it is hard to let go of the keyboard, letting someone else actually do the work and make the technical choices.

We now know that one of the most important factors in achieving first-rate problem solving through consensus is having neutral leadership. The position of discussion leader is so powerful that whoever leads or facilitates meetings and discussions must be assiduously neutral about the outcome in order that the best of what the group has to offer can emerge.

Such a leader is everyone's friend and nobody's advocate. Such a leader draws out the contributions of all without favoring any. Such a leader helps the group to build its own technical consensus without biasing the outcome or pushing a private agenda.

Ironically, what this means is that project managers and official team leaders are probably the worst choice for leading any discussions or meetings directed at technical problem solving and decision making. They have too much at stake. In a sense, they probably also know too much. The stronger they are as leaders, the more likely they are to actually dampen the free-spirited exploration of alternatives and the building of technical consensus that lead to the best results.

Some managers take a completely hands-off approach and try to sta
out of the technical problem solving altogether; however, this is not ideal fc
their teams, who are deprived of the manager's experience and expertise, c
for the managers, who miss out on much of the fun. The best of them will tur
over meetings and discussions to a neutral facilitator, then practice staying i
the background, learning how to contribute without dominating. Some ma
never learn how to do this, but many with whom I have worked actually enjo
being able to be "one of the bunch" again, taking part in technical discussior
on equal footing with the rest of the team.

There is life after promotion.

2

Consensus and Compromise[*]

Getting the most from a software development team depends on the ability to build technical consensus among the professionals on the project. But why should it matter whether you and your office mate agree on the layout of an entry form or the best way to report error messages? Technical consensus is not about getting along together or feeling close to your fellow programmers. (Not that there is anything wrong with getting along or feeling good about each other.) Technical consensus is about taking full advantage of all the skills and experiences of every team member. It's about building better software.

Software professionals may understand good software, or at least claim to know it when they see it, but technical consensus is a lot less well understood among developers. Probably most software developers have had some bad experiences with what they thought was design by consensus. They'll tell you tales of brilliant ideas being lost in discussions, about compromising their artistic integrity, about six-month projects that took years, and about groups that settled for less than the best. Listen carefully and you'll realize that what they are talking about is not consensus at all, but compromise. What's the difference?

Unpromising Compromise

Compromise is neither one thing nor another but something halfway in between, which often means in the middle of nowhere. Consider this variation

[*] From *Computer Language Magazine,* Volume 9, #4, April 1992.

on a classic example. Your team is designing a graphical user interface. One group strongly advocates placing the control buttons across the bottom of the screen, another is pushing for a panel down the left side. Between these horizontal and vertical extremes, a perfectly objective compromise can be struck just place the buttons along a diagonal across the middle of the screen!

A compromise, like this one, is frequently worse than any of the original alternatives, but a consensus solution can be better than all of them. Technical compromises often fail to account for the merits in each of the alternatives, and their advantages are lost by taking some kind of average position. True consensus is not based on compromise, in which everyone and every position loses a little, but on synthesis, in which everyone wins big. The payoff, of course, is better software.

A synthesis is something original that incorporates essential features of each contributing idea or proposal. In the interface design example given above, it's easy to see a creative synthesis in which the placement of the button panel is an option selectable by the user. Not only does a consensus based on synthesis incorporate the best of the alternatives, but new features or capabilities typically emerge from the combination. Out of the synthesis of horizontal and vertical button panels might emerge end-user customization. The product thus incorporates the best of both worlds, not the worst.

Building real consensus is not easy, as politicians and labor negotiators know all too well. Building a technical consensus is a little different from building political consensus, but it has some of the same elements. Both take a commitment to working things out; both require a certain faith in the process.

True Believers

Team members need to believe that it is possible to reach a technical synthesis incorporating the best elements and aspects of everyone's contributions. Believing this, they will stubbornly look for something better, rather than settle on compromise or cling needlessly to personal favorites. By persisting, they build their understanding of the problem and the nature of the strengths and weaknesses of each approach. From this, they enhance the odds of finding that creative something that exceeds them all.

Consensus design also works best when each of us believes that building a better piece of software is more important than getting our own favorite ideas into the result in some predetermined form. This investment in the quality of the outcome makes it easier to see the merits of whatever ideas emerge from the group process.

It helps, of course, if teamwork is applauded over individual pyrotechnics. Companies that reward individual performance instead of group success, or those that promote the lone wolf programmer over the team player, typically end up with a staff of uncompromising loners who probably will not and cannot play team sports. Such companies will rightly conclude that the best software is produced by their frontier-type geniuses. What they don't realize is that they've set it up to come out that way. Other outcomes are possible, of course.

One essential rule in building technical consensus is: No horse trading! Trading votes or support or influence is one of the classic tactics for political success, but it can destroy technical effectiveness. For example, we might work a trade in the interface design. I'll agree to your stupid idea of having the button panel across the bottom, if you agree to my clever design for icons without labels. The result is an interface that is less than the best in not one, but two features. Horse trading is just compromise in another disguise, but compromise made worse because decisions in one area contaminate those in another. Good technical consensus must see each issue as a separate problem, to be resolved on the merits, not as part of a point scoring system in which concessions in one area can be traded for obstinacy in another.

Just the Facts

One likes to think that technical decisions are made on the basis of technical issues — facts, measurable quantities, practical considerations. The truth is that feelings, opinions, intuition, and just plain biases are part of any decision-making or problem-solving process involving people. This is the reality of what it is to be human, and although some people try to deny, control, or suppress these nonrational aspects, it never works completely.

An essential skill of any team that hopes to build technical consensus is to learn to separate fact from opinion. If the group, collectively, is to make the best decisions and solve problems creatively, they need access to the best information and to know what kind of information they have. Opinions aren't bad; team members should be able to express them freely. Opinions can even be useful, especially when weighted by hard-won experience, but they must not be confused with facts or data or analyses. Facts, too, have their limitations. In the areas of aesthetics or marketing appeal, facts may be in short supply. Unfortunately, once some group members have made up their minds, they do not want to be bothered by facts.

Calling something a fact doesn't make it so, and groups have to learn to cut through the bull and agree not to abuse the language. My first wife learned in our early years to be suspicious of any statement I made that started with something like, "The facts in the matter clearly indicate ..." This was a warning that what followed was probably a bald-faced personal opinion unsupported by either data or evidence. Failing with this opening gambit, I was sometimes known to fall back on another tactic, which we came to know as the "Ninety-five-percent-of-all-scientists" move. Some of you may recognize it. "You know, the vast majority of professional software engineers, certainly more than ninety-five percent, favor this approach." Of course, to have any hope of continued effectiveness with this clever ruse, you have to vary the percentages. "Nearly seventy-eight percent of WordPerfect users know that the one best way is ..." "If we took a survey, better than two-thirds of C programmers would agree ..." Sometimes it seems that if you squint just right you can almost see those legions of scientists or software engineers or end users lining up behind the speaker to lend support to his or her position.

But that's just my opinion.

Negotiating Consensus*

You can't reach consensus unless you recognize it when you have it in your grasp. This means that software development groups trying to reach collective decisions are wise to agree, in advance, on the criteria by which technical matters will be decided. What is important? What matters? What is "good" and what is "bad" within the confines of this particular project?

Many times, when a group gets bogged down trying to reach a conclusion on an analysis or design problem and says, "We can't decide which way to go," I ask them, "How will you know which approach is better?" Engineering is about trade-offs — trading off a little more of this for somewhat less of that. Resolving trade-offs requires knowing something about the value, within a given project, of whatever is gained or lost in the trade-off.

In almost all engineering, projects are driven by competing criteria. It is not possible to meet all of them equally well in every detail at every juncture. Most projects pursue a mixture of technical and economic objectives. They want on-time delivery, run-time efficiency, ease of use, marketability, extensibility, and maintainability, along with a host of other goodies next to godliness. How are these to be weighed?

Straight Priorities

It helps to have your priorities straight. The metrics mavens will probably push you to reduce the decision criteria to a mathematical formula with weights and

---

* From *Computer Language Magazine*, Volume 9, #5, May 1992.

exponents for each factor, but this is generally neither necessary nor particularly useful. A simple rank ordering of the criteria is sufficient. During analysis and design, when most trade-offs are and should be resolved, we seldom, if ever, have enough data to quantify our assessments with any precision or confidence anyway. Plugging a bunch of seat-of-the-pants "guesstimates" into a bogus formula can give the dangerously deceptive appearance of disciplined objectivity. It can even become an escape hatch by which development teams avoid accountability. "Well, we just did what the formula said we should; it's not our fault that each screen update takes 17 seconds."

Accountability is promoted when development teams participate in establishing their principal goals and, on the basis of these, rank the criteria by which issues are to be decided. Once agreed upon, the criteria and their ordering are no longer open to debate. Most of the time they won't even enter into technical discussions. It is not necessary to analyze every little trade-off in terms of seven or eight criteria. The agreed-on list of criteria is taken off the shelf only when needed to help resolve a decision that is unclear or is taking too long.

Debate and Dialogue

Lack of clarity or agreement on criteria is not the only thing that can hinder negotiation to technical consensus. Free-wheeling discussions are not only the heart of consensus teamwork, but they're fun. Vigorous discussion, however, can cross the line into rancorous debate. Neither the courtroom nor the political podium offers a good model for consensus-based teamwork. Whether or not the adversarial approach works in the justice system, it is essential that design and development groups not end up as debating societies.

In one training class in object orientation, a member of a student design team complained to me that his group was getting nowhere. They were repeatedly getting bogged down in seemingly endless wrangles. Even what little progress they were able to make was seriously substandard compared to other teams in the same class.

As I watched them work — or try to work — I realized that the discussions were being dominated by one man who was an arguer par excellence, but his ideas were not up to his debating skills. Some other members of the team had a sense of the shortcomings in his thinking but, outgunned by his argumentation, kept falling back on opinions and feelings: "I don't think so." "It just doesn't feel right."

The original complainant had the motivation to see it work better, so I asked him to be group facilitator. His job had two parts: to make sure that no one person or side dominated the discussion, and to help the less active or less aggressive members articulate the real content and logic of their ideas.

If you are trying to build the best systems, you don't want to reduce technical solutions to whichever side can argue better, any more than you would want to base them on who has the most power or can shout the loudest. To avoid this, the power of logic and argumentation should belong to the group collectively, not to individuals or factions in a decision. The goal is to level the playing field so the merit of ideas and analyses in themselves carries the weight, not the cleverness of the argument or the loudness and long-windedness of the advocate.

If people can't seem to find a common ground arguing their own positions, one useful technique is to have advocates reverse roles and argue each other's positions. Or strong debaters can be assigned to argue the case of technically interesting but weakly defended notions. "Look, Mavis, you're good at this, so see if you can convince us about the real advantages of Greg's idea." Yet another twist is to say, "Let's apply this same line of reasoning to the other proposal."

Technical consensus is better thought of in terms of dialogue and negotiation than in terms of debate and argumentation. Some of the things that have been learned about negotiation in other areas can be very useful. Two excellent books from The Harvard Negotiation Project are highly recommended: *Getting to Yes* and *Getting Together* (Fisher and Ury 1981; Fisher and Brown 1988).

A perennial problem in negotiations is that the negotiating parties often come to the table already committed to a position, a proposal in which much thought and consideration may already have been invested. Instead of being genuinely open, each arrives with a predetermined solution. Negotiating from a position is thus a problem in itself. It tends to promote compromise at best, rather than consensus, and it is all too easy for things to degenerate into a shootout of one approach versus another.

Some of the simplest devices can make a big difference. The Harvard Negotiation Project learned that negotiations progressed better when disagreeing parties sat side-by-side, facing "their common problem," rather than facing each other over a table. I have found that placing factions in a technical dispute together facing a whiteboard or display screen can facilitate more productive discussions and speedier resolution.

Putting It Together

Sometimes starting from a set of prior proposals or already worked out solutions cannot be avoided. Two parts of the same company may have done prior work that we would not want to discount or waste, for example. Some companies even promote design competition in a kind of internal free market of ideas. When the time comes to build one system, usually the authors or competitors make their own pitch, introducing and describing their approaches. It can facilitate consensus building to have one person, someone who is less invested than the proponents, present all the alternatives before inviting the proposers into the discussion. Setting the right tone for what follows can help progress toward a consensus design. Participants can be encouraged to look for the strengths and advantages in other proposals before moving on to any critique. Realism about the starting positions can be encouraged: "Since it is more important for us to know about technical weaknesses in our systems than to pretend to have everything perfect, would each of you tell us about the weaknesses of your own approach?"

Where distinct subgroups or teams have been involved in preparing proposed solutions, after the initial discussions each subteam can be invited to go back and improve their own proposal by incorporating what they think are some of the best features of opposing approaches. This means that the next meeting starts with the opposing positions already moved closer together.

In general, technical consensus is built from alternatives by finding ways that combine or even transcend the best features of each. Instead of starting with positions, with specific technical proposals, it is often more efficient and effective to start with issues. The team's first job is to explore and settle on what are the essential technical issues represented in the various possibilities, the underlying reasons and technical rationale that are reflected in stated positions or proposed solutions.

The stage for creative synthesis is set even before the first meeting. Instead of having team members think about approaches to, say, the file structure, they might be asked to come with a catalog of the issues involved in designing an efficient file structure. They might list and prioritize specific decision criteria. They may even have to be discouraged from coming up with design ideas or proposed solutions. With many of the more maverick software developers, the problem is not so much spurring them on as reining them in before they stampede.

4

The Lowly and Exalted Scribe[*]

Remember Bob Cratchit toiling away on the books at the august firm of Scrooge and Marley, fingerless gloves on his hands to keep them from freezing between entries? I am a real nut about *A Christmas Carol* and was recently given a video of the marvelous black-and-white version starring Alistair Sims. Watching it started me to thinking about old Bob and all the other "clarks" who kept the records for so many enterprises over the centuries. These scribes were really the computers of their day. Without them, businesses would have been thrown into bankruptcy and whole industries cast into chaotic disarray. Their real power and importance went far beyond either their meager wages or their lowly status. If anything, what good old Bob and his compatriots did had more to do with the continued success of Scrooge and Marley than whatever Ebenezer contributed.

Things are hardly different today. Those who keep the records are held in low regard. Yet, in their pens and markers and keyboards can reside the power to spell success or failure for software development.

Software development groups, if they keep any records at all, are likely to limit their files and notes to results and conclusions, the work product or deliverables generated by their efforts. Programmers, especially, are loathe to write down anything other than the code itself unless they are threatened with a fine or imprisonment. Getting them to draw diagrams can be akin to getting an elephant to do pencil sketches. After all, isn't good code self-documenting?

[*] From *Computer Language Magazine,* Volume 9, #6, June 1992.

Vital Statistics

This view tends to lose sight of vital information. In general, when only the work product is preserved, we know what we got in the end but not how we got it. How the software was generated, the decisions along the way, are essential parts of the process. Do we want to trust to memory? Do we care only about our mistakes or do we also want to learn from them?

A particular problem with groups that keep only the end product of software development is that they do not preserve a record of what they didn't do. Often it can be as important to know what approaches were rejected and for what reasons as to know which were selected. This is vital information to have when it comes to future versions or systems or to preserve for when the current system goes down the tubes.

You have probably had occasion to examine some of your own code some years or months after you wrote it. Have you ever had the experience of spotting something that you just knew must be wrong and you wondered how the software ever squeaked by without crashing because of it? If you gave in to the temptation to "correct" such a latent bug, as I have on occasion, then you may have found that "fixing" it brought the system to its knees. The problem, of course, is that the code only *looked* wrong, but the code did not explain why it was actually right. It does not help to have a comment in the code like the one I once saw that read, "Do not change this decision; it looks wrong but is really right." If the programmer knew why it was right and why the alternative was wrong, then why wasn't that logic recorded in the comment? We need to know what alternatives were considered and rejected and why if we are going to be able to maintain a system for years or build its successor five years later after all the original development staff are long gone.

Business consultants today talk about organizational learning as a key to enterprise success over the long run. Organizations, like individuals, can learn from their experiences, accumulating knowledge and improving performance. To the extent that organizational learning resides solely in the brains of individual employees, the organization is vulnerable. Employees get sick, take vacations, and change jobs. They forget.

In truth, the learnings of an organization are embodied in its records, its policies, and its practices or processes, not solely in its people. The more we document and record what happens as we go along, the more likely such learning is to survive the group or team that produced it.

Scribbles

Enter the lowly scribe. Fanfares and cheers!

The function of the scribe or recorder on a software development team is to be responsible for the team's collective memory, the repository of its work product as well as of the processes that generated the results. The scribe keeps the books. In the Structured Open teamwork model devised independently by Rob Thomsett and myself (Constantine 1989, 1991a; Thomsett 1990), the role is referred to as Information Manager. This newspeak title is intended to raise the status of the role, somewhat akin to the ad for a garbage truck driver calling the job a "sanitation transport engineer."

It is easy to see the scribe in a meeting as a mere functionary, hardly more than a human dictaphone, but this position actually draws on many skills. You can't keep effective notes on things you don't understand, so software scribes have to be fully trained developers. And they must know how to record and manage information for a real development project. The quality of the records determines the quality of the group's permanent collective memory of what happened and how. A scribe who captures a full account of what the group did, complete but without excessive detail, well organized and understandable, is a team member worth his or her weight in C++ code.

A good group memory must carry a lot of information. Some of this is volatile or temporary storage, some is permanent. Some of it is active and worked with dynamically in meetings and the day-to-day tasks of the team, while some is more passively filed. The information management functions can be divided for convenience into session memory and project memory. Session memory consists of the records generated and manipulated during group sessions, whenever the team is meeting and solving problems as a group. Project memory covers the permanent records and documentation produced and used by the group. It includes the work product, which means not only code but also all the design and analysis models and documents generated along the way to the code. Project memory also covers inputs to the project, such as requirements and specifications, and other background documents. Managing the project memory really requires a librarian, and often the role is known by that title.

Modular Memory

An essential part of the session memory is the process record, a log of the discussions and decisions made by the group (Doyle and Strauss 1982). The idea of keeping process records is probably new to most software development groups, but it has been a part of meeting management for decades. In creating a process record, new scribes tend to fall into one of two traps. Either they try to write down everything as if they were taking dictation, or they wait until the group reaches some conclusion and just summarize. For technical teamwork, a "he-said/she-said" kind of record is neither necessary nor ideal. A good process record keeps track of key events along the way to an outcome, especially the alternatives considered, decisions made, and arguments presented. These are essential contributors to group learning and may be invaluable when it comes time for a project "post mortem" or design review.

For software development, a continuous and unstructured process record is not ideal. Some categories of information are so commonly generated by development teams working in collaborative sessions that they warrant separate recording for special attention. It is useful to keep a "do-list" for noting those things that come up in discussions but are not acted on right away. This alone can justify the frustration of keeping session records because it can save projects from those embarrassing oversights that tend to show up in systems integration or after product shipment. "Oops, I thought we took care of that dangling pointer problem!"

A good session memory also records deferred decisions, which are best kept separate from the heap on the "do-list." A formal storage place for deferred decisions can also speed up decision making. Instead of wasting time with endless discussion driven by inadequate understanding or missing information, the group can put the issue on the deferred decisions list. Often, by the time the group returns to the issue, enough has been learned to make a swift decision. A third special record that proves useful on development teams is a "parts bin," where bits and pieces of bright technical ideas or partial solutions can be set aside temporarily without disrupting the main thread of discussion. The "reject bin" is just the opposite, a place to note all those unused ideas and paths not taken, along with that vital rationale for rejection.

All four of these special records — the do-list, the deferred decisions, the parts bin, and the reject bin — serve to record things that might otherwise be lost or forgotten. They also help the group to make efficient use of time. By recording digressions and distractions in one of these specialized bins, the group can stay on track with the main problem without losing useful information. It can also keep a group from getting stuck on discussions that are going nowhere. Instead of more wheel-spinning, an issue can be moved to one of the "bins" for later attention. The bins themselves also serve as quality assurance mechanisms. By the end of a project, everything in the bins must have been crossed off or otherwise accounted for.

So who is the lucky person who gets to be a scribe? Some approaches, such as *Joint Application Design* (Wood and Silver 1989), bring in outside facilitators and scribes, trained specialists who are good at it and can free up project members to concentrate on creating software solutions. Some groups permanently assign the job to one person on the team, often a junior member or trainee. For most software development teams, a compromise between these approaches can be more effective. The function of information management can belong to the team as a whole, with the actual responsibility rotated among members of the project team. No one is exempted from playing the scribe, but no one is stuck with the job for too long. The job of Session Recorder is one that may actually change from moment to moment with the flow of the meeting, or it may stay in one set of capable hands for an entire working session. However, for the sake of sanity and good teamwork, it probably should switch at least with each new meeting. In longer meetings, it probably should rotate at least every hour or so. The truth is that being a good scribe takes extraordinary concentration, and very few people on the planet actually enjoy the role.

Taking care of the archives, the off-line or project memory, can be rotated less frequently. Passing the torch on a daily basis would only ensure chaos or nonperformance. During a one-year project, the overall job, what might be termed the Project Information Manager or Project Scribe, might change hands only once or twice at the most.

So, take a scribe to lunch. Next week it could be you.

5

Official Space[*]

Your office mate chews gum, plays "Where-in-the-World-is-Carmen-San-Diego?" on his desktop machine, and interrupts with burps, groans, and stupid questions whenever you are trying to logic your way through some obscure bug. You've been with the company several years and feel it's high time you had a private office. You go to your boss saying you need more room and more freedom from distracting noise and interruptions. You say it's cost effective, that if you had more space and fewer distractions you'd be more productive. You mention studies to prove it. You need at least a hundred square feet of dedicated work space and thirty square feet of desk-and-table-top. A window would be good, too. In Denmark they legislate that you inform your boss. In Denmark she would have to give you a window.

In the folk wisdom of software development, more space, more quiet, and fewer interruptions yields higher programming productivity with fewer defects. A hundred square feet of office and thirty square feet of work surface has become the plea of programmers around the world. This notion was made a permanent part of industry folklore by Tom DeMarco and Tim Lister in their 1987 classic, *Peopleware*. Drawing on several sources, but primarily their own annual "coding war games," they concluded that programmers with privacy, more elbow room, and more space to spread out their diagrams and listings were more productive.

---

[*] From *Software Development,* Volume 1, #12, December 1993.

Shaping Process

At work, at home, in a restaurant, or in a classroom, physical space shapes what happens and can happen among people. At a long banquet table you may be able to converse with a couple of people on either side and a few across from you, but it's not likely that you'll be able to carry on a meaningful exchange with anyone clear down on the other end. King Arthur made his table round as a statement about equality. It also made it easier for all the knights to talk with each other.

How buildings or offices are designed and furnished can have a powerful effect on communication and collaboration. I once lived in an apartment building for two full years but met few of the neighbors. The entryway of the building was a tiny little airlock, barely big enough for one person and a bag of groceries; the halls were narrow, dark, and sterile. There was simply no place for people to bump into each other, no place for serendipitous interaction.

Offices do not usually suffer from tiny entrances and gloomy hallways, but modern high-tech offices have their equivalent architectural inhumanities. The flexible-partition, open-office design dominates modern office layout. Despite its appealing name, the system is usually neither flexible nor open.

One computer company has buildings with miles of corridors crisscrossing acres of cubicles, all marked out by those sand-colored acoustic partitions that make you crane your neck to see over but that merely dampen conversations to the distracting murmur of an opera house just before curtain time. There's not only no privacy, but there's not much that's open, either. People in offices separated by more than twenty feet in this beige warren can go for years without ever crossing paths. Visitors have to be escorted — not for security reasons but to keep them from becoming lost. Mail stops have designations like KK14-HDQ:117N\BB.R3, an arcane code referenced to floors, pillars, and rows. The flexibility of flexible office layout is largely illusory. Moving a partition would require uprooting and rerouting ethernet and telco cables, to say nothing of revamping mail-stop designations. The walls may be flexible, but the mailroom personnel are decidedly not.

From the standpoint of using office space to leverage developer productivity, these inflexible "flexible" systems are usually laid out to be about as bad as anyone could devise. They do not make it easy to work alone, and they do not make it easy to work together. They do not make it easy to get away or to meet casually.

The whole story on office layout and developer productivity is more complex than just more space and more isolation. First, there is that old bugaboo of all social science research, the cause-and-correlation conundrum. The high performers in the coding war games may have had bigger offices and fewer distractions *because* they were high performers, not vice versa. Or their performance may have contributed to their companies' ability to afford quieter and more spacious facilities.

Even more important, the findings reported in the DeMarco and Lister book were based on coding and testing, not on the complete process of software development. Their annual competitions required that each competitor work alone — no teamwork. So space and quiet seem to support isolated coders, but what about collaborative teams?

Collaborative Communication

For efficient collaboration, project teams do need space: space of their own as a team, space laid out to their needs as a team. The best evidence points to the need for a mix of open and closed spaces for smooth collaboration. Offices should support groups of two or three people working together intensively for shorter or extended periods and have at least one locale for meetings of the entire project staff. If there is no place where the entire team can meet comfortably, building the team into a cohesive working unit will be much harder.

One software manager ardently supported project teamwork but was disappointed with the quality of collaboration among his software developers. The floor where they worked was a fun-house maze of narrow corridors with tiny little glass-walled offices — isolated but not private. Few offices were big enough for two, and those that were large enough often held office mates who were assigned to different projects. I observed one team scheduled for a meeting in the largest conference room on the floor. Eleven developers crammed into a room that held a conference table and six chairs with about seven inches clearance all around. Between the end of the table and a small whiteboard was barely room for the team leader to pace and turn. Needless to say, the meeting was brief.

One crucial office need of collaborative teams is a common meeting space dedicated to the team "for the duration." They need a place to serve as headquarters, a "situation room" where the whole team can convene for meetings and discussions and a protected territory where members can retreat from outside distractions and interference. Intermittent use of a conference room shared with various others is a poor substitute.

A dedicated project "situation room" of sufficient size is especially important for teams using "system storyboarding" (Zahniser 1990, 1993) and other group analysis and design approaches. The walls and whiteboards of the team HQ become the repository for the group's work, its visible, external "group memory," preserving essential parts of the work product and the process through which it evolves. The walls of the team HQ might be covered with everything from the team flag and mission statement to essential design documents. The room and its decorations become part of the team culture, contributing to a sense of shared identity that helps members work together smoothly and efficiently.

When team members are split between buildings, spread across different sites, or scattered around the globe, collaboration — even communication — becomes more difficult and more expensive. Other things being equal, spreading a project among multiple sites — even just different buildings or different floors — can add as much as 50–100% to the cost. Because spatially distributed project teams will almost invariably be less efficient than comparable groups at a single site, dispersed teams need compensating mechanisms. Good e-mail and teleconferencing facilities can help, but nothing can substitute for coming together to meet face-to-face and press the flesh at least once.

Back in the dark ages of software engineering when I was at M.I.T., studies of engineering and R&D groups had established that productivity improved with better communication and that communication improved when groups worked in the right environment. The best arrangements had central open spaces that facilitated or even forced engineers to bump into each other. Buildings with fixed walls and management with closed minds can be deterrents, but creative compromises are possible. Risa Hyman describes one group that made inventive use of the conventional string of offices arrayed along a central corridor (Hyman 1993). The hallway itself was outfitted with whiteboards along the walls and was used as the primary meeting space!

Having the right physical layout can help teamwork, but it's up to managers and team members to determine whether walls become barriers or bridges to more effective teamwork.

6

Irksome Interruptions[*]

Interruptions can be irksome. On the other hand, a bug that doesn't come to your attention may stay in the code, and an idea that you never hear about won't help you solve a problem. How well and how efficiently people communicate within an office or on a project team can make a real difference in performance. Sharing an office makes it easy to share information. Sometimes that's a plus, sometimes not. The kind of intense and focused thinking that is necessary for good code construction or for ferreting out elusive bugs benefits from sustained and undivided attention. When the words of an article or the lines of code just seem to flow from the fingertips, the last thing you want is someone throwing in a casual comment about something Robert X. Cringely wrote. At other times, the fresh perspective of someone else's off-hand remark may get you thinking along new lines. Sometimes, talking through a design with an attentive listener can help you see what is missing or where hidden problems might lurk.

Good office teamwork requires easy access without irritation. People who work together or share the same working space have many legitimate reasons to interrupt each other: asking for help, tossing out ideas, checking on status, and, in general, coordinating the work at hand. On the other hand, uninterrupted time to think and create is essential. An ill-timed interruption can erase a great idea, kick an elusive thought just out of reach, or make you lose track completely within a complicated line of reasoning.

* From *Software Development*, Volume 2, #6, June 1994.

This problem isn't new and isn't special to software development groups, but developers may have advantages in coming up with better ways to manage group communication. Of course, computer people love to solve social and organizational problems by using computers, so the first thing that probably comes to mind is a fast network with fancy e-mail facilities. But sometimes a very simple system can go a long way. Maybe all that is needed is some better vocabulary.

Word Warriors

Technical fields often have a rich interaction with ordinary vocabulary. The computer field has usurped many everyday words for narrow technical purposes. We have taken over "object" and "entity," leaving nothing to refer to those ordinary things in the physical world around us. We've appropriated "method" and "message," arrogated "protocol" and "file." It works the other way, too, of course. Technical terms enter the mainstream to the point that computer jargon now peppers conversations on the street.

Tech weenies in the computer field have a special passion for interpolating their jargon into ordinary conversation, extending and expanding the meaning of the terminology to cover social purposes. They struggle to "parse" a garbled voice-mail message or maniacally "multiplex" two conversations. Habitual patterns of behavior are "hard coded" in "ROM." Programmers will "port" a tape deck from one car to another rather than buy a new one. They will do a "core dump" to write a first rough draft of a report on yesterday's design meeting. This can get pretty tedious or sound awfully silly, but technobabble occasionally enriches ordinary language in useful or interesting ways.

I remember my first experience with an attempt to import programming terminology into conversation management. Our group was experimenting with commercial applications of Lisp and became so enamored with the language that we talked in lists and dotted pairs. Our conversations became punctuated by oddball exclamations. We'd "cons" two ideas together and "car" and "cdr" our way through conversation so multithreaded that eventually someone would complain of stack overflow and call for garbage collection. For those of you who never learned to thpeak with a lithp, "car" means "the first thing off the list" or "the left branch" while "cdr" (pronounced "could-er") means "the rest of the list" or "the right branch." The funny names have stayed with Lisp, even though they refer to hardware registers in the long defunct IBM 709/ 7090/7094 computers, namely "contents of address register" and "contents of decrement register."

Our short-lived affectation probably sounded pretty dorky and wasn't terribly useful, except in helping us to learn the jargon and anchor the concepts of Lisp firmly in our minds. I haven't "cadadr-ed" an idea in decades. If you hang around our offices nowadays, though, you're apt to hear some equally weird but maybe more useful idiomatic interjections.

Office Protocol

The usual ways of interrupting in polite society are just too long and clumsy for efficient collaboration. "Excuse me. Are you busy? I hope you don't mind. I just have a quick question. It will only take a second." A second? It has already taken six and a half! By this point, the interruption is a *fait accompli*. By the time your brain has parsed and processed all that noise and reached a decision on what to do about it, you've forgotten which line of code you were looking at and which method of which subclass you were intending to invoke.

Working groups need a vocabulary of interruptions that is short, sweet, and simple. What works for hardware seems to work for people, so in our offices we IRQ, we ACK, and we NAK.

"IRQ" is short for "interrupt request"; it's pronounced, appropriately, "irk." As in "I'd like to irk you?" All you need say is just the one word, "IRQ?" A rising intonation makes it more polite, an explosive final consonant makes it more imperative. The word is sharp enough to penetrate through the hiss of cooling fans and the whine of laser printers, yet it's short enough to barely deflect your mental processes. The possible responses are "ACK" or "NAK" (pronounced "ack" and "en-ack" or "nack"), meaning, "Okay, go ahead!" or "Not now!" respectively. You barely have to be conscious of your surroundings to burp out either an ACK or a NAK. Both ACK and NAK have an appropriate phonetic flavor that seems to fit with the situation of being interrupted.

The interrupt protocol is simplicity itself. An interrupter says "IRQ!" and waits for a response. The interrupted person may continue for a short time before completing the handshaking, perhaps marking a spot in the text, completing a title box, or making a quick note about what they were doing. As soon as they are ready to service the interrupt, they respond by saying "ACK." A response of "NAK" means, "No, don't interrupt me now." We regard it as a polite version of "Go away. Don't bug me!" All this may seem too silly for words, but it is remarkable how such a simple system can contribute to smoother resource sharing in a working group. Although we haven't found the need for it in day-to-day work, an obvious extension would be to provide for an occasional "NMI" (pronounced "nimmy"), that is, a "nonmaskable interrupt." Good etiquette would save "NMI" for true emergencies or top-priority issues that justify grabbing the full foreground processing capacity of your poor colleague's wetware CPU. The recommended protocol would be to pause briefly before beginning to talk, although no ACK or NAK is required.

People who IRQ you more often than necessary are dubbed, appropriately, IRQsome. These you deal with by doing your Bill-the-Cat impersonation, loudly crying, "ACK, NAK. NAK! ACK!" while tearing at your hair. If you can come up with a fur ball at the right moment, it's all the more effective.

End of interrupt.

II

Cowboys and Cowgirls

Introduction

One of the great things about doing a column in a computer magazine is that readers respond by electronic mail, creating a lively immediacy in the relationship between reader and writer. Over the years, *Peopleware* has generated a steady exchange with an intelligent and interested readership who frequently and repeatedly get excited or incensed enough to inquire or comment. I have come to look at reading the regular e-mail (and irregular snailmail) as a part of writing the column.

I was totally unprepared, however, for the deluge triggered by my first column on "coding cowboys." In fact, that column and its successor broke records for reader response. Suddenly, I was in the wild west of an earlier epoch. For the intensity of reaction, I might as well have been talking with hunters about gun control or cattle ranchers about charging for grazing rights on public lands. Some of the "flaming" that swept over the electronic prairie was too intense for verbatim reproduction in a family-oriented publication like *Software Development*. Clearly, the issue touched some archetypal anarchy among software developers. My vocabulary grew as I caught some of the more trendy insults of the electronic age and was surprised to learn that "commie pinko" was still in the lexicon of contempt of some programmers. *Plus c'est change, plus c'est même chose.*

The topic turned out to be a rich enough lode to be mined in multiple columns and a full-length article. Along the way I made some friends and I probably made some enemies. And I will most probably never get an invitation to lunch in Redmond with "The Bill."

7

Cowboy Coders*

The millennium arrived and you didn't even know it! Software reliability became, at long last, a reality. And how was this breakthrough in software engineering achieved? I quote from a 16-page marketing blurb from Nanomush, Inc., mailed to millions of benighted users and developers: "One of the most powerful additions to Blerbbleflox 3.1 is 'parameter validation.' Parameter validation means that when information is passed from an application to the Blerbbleflox operating system, Blerbbleflox checks the information to make sure it is valid." What a novel idea! Why didn't you think of that, eh?

This bit of attempted self-congratulation revealed that Nanomush, one of the world's largest developers of languages and operating environments, had finally begun to practice the rudiments of sound software engineering, techniques so basic that those worthy of the name programmer have known and practiced them since shortly after they learned to code. Could this cast some light on the shortcomings of earlier releases of similar software? But we should rejoice rather than carp, lauding the efforts of all fledgling software engineers,

---

* From *Computer Language Magazine*, Volume 9, #8, August 1992.

encouraging them to continue to mature, perhaps even to try to learn about coupling and cohesion or information hiding.

One wonders how the computer world arrived at this sorry state of affairs in systems software until one looks more closely at the character of the developers responsible for some of the products on which we depend so much. My colleagues who deal with organizational dynamics would call them "cowboys." Cowboys, the last of the rugged and untamable individualists, are found in various fields, but nowadays many of them are punching assembly language cattle on the silicon frontier. Please note that the sobriquet ends in "boys" not "men."

In the spring of 1992, at Miller Freeman's Software Development Conference, I found myself part of a panel on the putative topic of "structured" versus "unstructured" management of software development. I was paired with one of the development managers from Nanomush. His position, wholly on the side of the cowboys, was that what kept programmers from reaching their full potentials were managers who tried to impose standards, expectations, or restrictions. Just get out of the way and let them programmers do their thing. Structured methods, disciplined development, paper-and-pencil model building, and software metrics are all unjustified impositions on the free artistic expression of our brilliant programming cowboys. No wonder there is such unpredictable performance and variability in quality within the products being shipped by such companies.

Why does it take four releases and 12,000 (no kidding) beta test sites to discover that something less cryptic than "unrecoverable application error; okay?" is needed? But cowboys don't like to be reined in by specific quality criteria or by being expected to think out in advance what is really needed. No, let's just jump into that old development corral and cut some code, wranglers! The GUI may be pretty and the coding clever — after all, we are artistic geniuses — but to hell with real usability or reliability; those might require planning or, heaven forbid, discipline.

And we need not single out any one software company in this regard; the market abounds with countless examples. It is rare, however, when promotional literature or panel presentations give us such candid glimpses into the maturity of developers and their development methods.

Maverick Maturity

Maturity is a central issue for the field of software development. Methodologists are wondering how long it will take for software engineering to mature as a discipline, managers are concerned about the level of "process maturity" in the approaches to development used within their organizations, and project leaders wonder about the maturity of the individuals whom they are called on to lead.

One large corporation surveyed their software development groups to determine how much and at what level of sophistication groups were making use of established systematic or disciplined software engineering approaches. The most advanced in their use of software engineering methodologies were the MIS and business information departments. Engineering support groups were intermediate in their use. Rock bottom last were — you guessed it — the people who wrote the operating systems, compilers, and utility software. Surveys of CASE tool penetration show similar patterns. Where engineering discipline and process maturity count most, software development is a wild-west side show dominated by coding cowboys.

Our culture lionizes the lone genius who does everything from start to finish on the development of some brilliant theory or machine or piece of software, but the truth is, nobody really makes it on their own. Even the eremitic teenaged hacker, cranking out code in the isolation of his bedroom on the machine he assembled himself, is dependent on the army of engineers who designed and built the chips, the legions of programmers who went before to create the tools. For those who are monitoring my LSI (Latent Sexism Index), it is not accidental that I use the masculine pronoun here. Most young hackers are male, and the particular mentality associated with cracking on-line computer systems or hacking clever new worms to bring networks to their knees is almost exclusively a male psychopathology. Boys also commit the majority of vandalism, and let's face it, writing viruses or trashing corporate files or invading government computers is just vandalism, nothing more. Unfortunately, it is only a matter of time before such computer vandalism results in loss of life; we've already come close on several occasions.

Coeducation

So, how did we get, in just a few paragraphs, from software engineering and methodological maturity to these gender issues? Because, at the heart of it, the immaturity of the cowboy mentality that shuns discipline and collaboration alike is largely a male thing.

At one meeting of a planning group within a software company, the assembled "team" went through 40 minutes of the men playing competitive games, debating definitions, jockeying for position, showing off their knowledge and erudition, and generally trying to score points off each other. Slowly, one by one, the men drifted away, excusing themselves with one rationale or another, usually something ostensibly "more important" having to do with "real work." When only women were left, one of them said, "Now, we can get something done." They wrapped up the real job of the meeting quickly and efficiently, while enjoying themselves in the process.

Of course it's a stereotype, but let's face it, guys, women understand collaboration a lot better than we do. For whatever reasons, little boys compete and little girls collaborate. Females, as a rule, are much better at building relationships, supporting and motivating each other. (So, one wonders why more of them aren't managers and project leaders in our field. Think about it, you middle and upper managers: all other things being equal, a female may have a decided edge over a male as a team leader — even with those Neanderthal programmers who claim they can't work for a woman.)

In my years as a marriage and family therapist I came, reluctantly, to the conclusion that most modern men basically do not know all that much about parenting, or, for that matter, relationships in general. This is not a matter of male bashing, just one of those statistical facts of life. I've been lucky to know uncommon males who really understood about *relating*, and I've also known my share of interpersonally inept females. Neither sex has a monopoly on either sensitivity or relationship bungling. But the odds favor women, at least in most cultures, when it comes to finesse with the people issues.

Now I expect to hear it loud and long from all those coding cowboys out there who insist that rugged individualism and the free market of programming independence are the only hope for American business (or humankind, if they're less provincial in their outlook). These are precisely the ones who insist that working collaboratively cramps their style, that building consensus drags them down to the lowest common denominator, that having to design before they code slows them down. Strange that so many of them produce such ordinary software or even fundamentally flawed systems.

True, there are some scattered few, women and men alike, with the genius, the vision, the talent, and the creativity to go it alone and do credible and laudable work. For most of us, though, releasing our real potential lies in learning how to build off each other's ideas in a creative synthesis that goes beyond what each of us might be capable of doing alone. *Our* work is likely to be better than either *my* work or *your* work.

So, grow up, cowboys. Learn how to stand on each other's shoulders instead of each other's toes. And, please, all the women out there, lend us a hand. We have so much to learn.

8

Cowboy Homecoming*

When I first rode out onto the software range to write about the problem of "cowboy coders," I had no idea what a hornet's nest I was poking. Cowboy coders are those industry denizens who denigrate discipline of any kind, spurning methods and models and management alike. They would rather quit than cooperate. The thought of designing before cutting code is enough to make them feel downright claustrophobic. My suggestion that these mostly male code punchers might learn from their more collaborative female counterparts triggered a dust storm of protests. The protesters, nearly all male themselves, accused me of everything from sexism to communism, so it should not be surprising that I held off returning to the subject for a spell. But circumstances seem to impel me once more to think about the untamed wilds of the programming frontier.

For starters, my younger daughter graduated from college. Commencement was filled with its Kodak moments. I remember particularly that swell of paternal pride as she received her degree in psychology, then the relief-filled realization that the last of a long series of distressingly large checks had been posted to the college. And I remember the commencement speech.

Chimp Tales

Commencement speeches are rarely memorable. They're usually either pious, platitudinous, or political; some particularly deadly ones may be all three. But Wheaton's new president had prevailed on a former Cornell colleague to help

---

* From *Software Development,* Volume 1, #10, October 1993.

launch her first Wheaton graduating class. Carl Sagan filled his remarks with wit and intelligence and kept them brief. Inspired by the graduating class, only the second to go through four years of coeducation at Wheaton, Sagan started by looking at gender and behavior. He focused on women and men and the world they make for themselves by first turning the spotlight onto chimpanzees. Chimps, of course, are our genetic brothers and sisters; 99.6% of the active genes are identical in chimps and humans. The behavior of chimps and humans is not all genetics, of course, but neither is it all simply learned. Just as looking at our own parents can tell us something about ourselves, we can learn something about *homo sapiens sapiens* by looking in the mirror of our primate relatives.

When stressed by crowded conditions, male chimps grow increasingly aggressive and competitive, gathering rocks to throw and keeping other males at a distance. Sagan described a male chimp, arms loaded with rocks, confronted by a quiet female blocking his way. Slowly, gently, she pries open the fingers of his clenched fists and deposits the rocks on the ground, then walks away. For some males, this is enough, and they turn to other chimpish interests, but a few just don't get it. Slower to learn, they have to be gently disarmed a number of times before they get the message. It reminded me of some of the men I know.

Sagan returned from chimpanzees to the subject of people and the widely demonstrated differences in how little boys and little girls play, the tendency for women to promote cooperation where men are prone to compete. He wondered whether the world might be more collaborative if women had truly equal access to positions of power and influence. Not a few senators and token female CEOs, but an honest fifty-fifty split of the leadership pie.

And I wondered where Carl Sagan was last year when I needed him, when I was being pelted by troops of software chimps, males all, for saying many of the same things. I guess they must have felt crowded by talk of cooperative coding.

If all cowboy coders were lone rangers, they would not present so many problems. Many of them are darned good. In isolation, on self-contained applications, cowboys can turn in whirlwind performances. Even one or two on a larger team can spice up a development project. Managed with judicious attention to the software interfaces and personal connections, cowboys can add diversity in ideas and perspectives without undermining the integrity of the system.

Unfortunately, cowboys have been known to gather not only at rodeos and roundups but also at large software houses, where they create complex system software — with the emphasis on complex. It seems just possible that some of the slipped schedules and bug-ridden software that plague our industry might be related to the wild-hair programming practices of undisciplined cowboy coders and the maverick managers who encourage them.

Cowboy coders can be creative, no doubt. That's not always a good thing. In the system software on which everything else depends we want peerless performance and, at the bottom of it all, rock-solid reliability. Performance can sometimes be bought through cowboy tactics, but reliable software generally comes from the discipline that cowboys disdain. Code that's both fast and flawless requires the very best software engineering practices carried out with consistent rigor.

Lots of cowboys also means lots of code — whether it's needed or not. It means great quantities of unstructured code, conceived on the fly and created independently, all of it different, all of it with the unique stamp of some cowboy's personal style.

Trail Bosses

Imagine, if you will, trying to produce a major new operating system, not with a closely coordinated team of disciplined professionals, but with a couple hundred coding cowboys. It's tough enough to lead a small posse of cowboys. Imagine trying to manage a whole ranch full of them. It might take a lot just to get their attention.

Perhaps, then, we should sympathize with the head of the Windows NT project who harangued his herd continually and even reportedly punched a hole in an office wall. Maybe as an ex-programmer with a reputation for clever code he understood the maverick mentality.

Alas, understanding may not be enough. As described by the *Wall Street Journal* (26 May 1993), the entire project seemed doomed to produce a gargantuan, overly complicated, and defect-ridden result. With some 200 programmers furiously cutting code to specs generated on the fly, the project promoted a cacophonous free-for-all.

Like the cattlemen and sheep herders of yore, coders and testers were turned into competing camps, pitted against each other in pitched battles. Such a division of labor can be effective in reducing software defects. But in the project pecking order, coders — mostly male and mostly cock-sure — came first. When coders complained that testers were trying too hard, the testers were overruled, presumably in the interest of meeting deadlines or performance goals.

With schedules slipping and problems proliferating, the NT staff went into "ship mode" — and stayed there for nearly two solid years. Since error rates rise when humans are fatigued and stressed, long hours under pressure will only multiply the number of defects injected into code. Some weeks they were finding and "fixing" on the order of a thousand bugs. But, even the best regression testing protocols detect only a fraction of injected bugs. The undiscovered residue of all those long weekdays and weekends awaits future users.

There are alternatives. Discipline works. As reported by Al Pietresanta at the 1989 Software Development Conference in Boston, by using "clean room" coding techniques and continuous process improvement, coding defects even in very large systems can be cut to less than one in ten thousand lines of code.

Maturity pays off. Large projects carried out by mature organizations using mature processes have been found to cut development costs by factors of 20–30 compared with more free-form hack-and-slash approaches.

There may be many bastions of coding cowboyism, but in the case of Rancho Redmond, it's now a matter of record. Mitchell Duncan, chief builder on the NT project, is quoted by the *Journal* as saying, "We have all these cowboy developers, just slinging code like crazy."

And sling they did — 4.3 million lines worth. Just be careful where you step.

9

Team Harmony[*]

What does it take to be a leader? What kind of leadership leads to effective teamwork and successful problem solving? Back in the late 1970s, British management consultant R. Meredith Belbin (1976) was asked by the Administrative Staff College in England to find answers to just these questions through formal observations and experiments.

Using the best scientific knowledge and thinking of the day, he assembled experienced middle to senior managers into teams to take part in competitive activities that could be objectively rated. Beginning with an "A-Team" that brought together the best and the brightest, the truly outstanding performers, he assigned participants to various teams until there remained only an assortment of leftovers who did not seem to fit with any of the carefully defined high-performance teams. These last he threw together to form one last team, a motley crew of undistinguished misfits.

At the end of extensive tests and exercises, the teams were ranked on their objective performance. To the surprise of all, the all-star team ended up dead last in the rankings, while the motley crew topped the charts.

Required Roles

Careful study of the results revealed that the key ingredient was diversity. Teams whose members showed greater diversity in leadership style per-

[*] From *Computer Language Magazine*, Volume 9, #9, September 1992.

formed better, while teams whose members all showed basically similar ways of leading and participating within the group performed less well. Going back to his observations and data on the team members, Belbin identified eight distinct "leadership roles" or team functions that team members seemed to play in the most diversified, most successful teams.

Belbin's leadership roles represent functions needed by a team for peak performance, and they also represent styles in which those leadership functions can be carried out. Four of these resemble conventional notions of how real leaders behave. A *driver* is a team member who typically defines things, steering and shaping the team thinking and the discussion toward a particular end or outcome, imposing specific patterns of work or approaches. We all know drivers in this sense, and often they are people seen as dominant in teams. But there are other important forms of team leadership. An *originator* is a leader in ideas, an innovator and inventor who advances new ideas or approaches. A *coordinator* is a leader in terms of process, a facilitator who helps move the problem solving forward by drawing on the entire team as human resources. A *monitor* is an evaluator who applies critical review and analysis to the group work, in effect; a leader in quality assurance.

The other four roles that Belbin regarded as forms of legitimate leadership are more often thought of as supporting roles. In fact, one of them is sometimes called just that. A *supporter* provides emotional leadership, fostering team spirit and nurturing team members as individuals. An *implementer* leads in transforming concepts and plans into practical systems and solutions, carrying out group plans as agreed. A *finisher* sees that work of the group is completed and maintains the group's focus and sense of urgency. An *investigator* manages the interfaces with other groups and resources, exploring and conducting research.

For the highest performance, team leadership is a multifaceted function. Typically, the varied forms of essential leadership are distributed among team members rather than being concentrated into one "superleader" who can do it all. Indeed, this "shared leadership" model has been found as the hallmark of more successful groups of many kinds.

Two distinct senses of diversity are essential to effective teamwork. High-performance teams need varied technical skills and backgrounds. This seems to be the easy part for most people. From diverse experiences and abilities the team is able to cover more of the technical landscape than one person ever could. Of course, there are always those superstars who are driven to try to do it all and be expert at everything, but scant few are very successful. The price of too many interests is often a sacrifice in depth or rigor, and the dilettante risks being singled out for criticism. (There are some who have opined, for instance, that the eclectic and versatile author of this book is really just "intellectually promiscuous.")

In addition to diverse skills and knowledge, Belbin's work — and numerous other studies that followed — suggests that variety in *style* is at least as important as variety in content. By style I mean not only personality, but also interpersonal proclivities. If everyone is trying to lead the way through the door, the entire team jams up at the jamb. If everyone is of the sort who looks for something to play off of before committing support, the entire crew may end up waiting at the bottom of the stairs while the plane takes off without them.

Liking Alikes

These findings pose some challenges for software developers. One difficulty is that most everybody seems to prefer to work with people who are essentially like themselves, while better team performance seems to result from putting together people who are essentially different. Having a variety of skills and a variety of working styles in which to carry out those skills gives team flexibility.

I think of this matter of team diversity as not unlike ethnic diversity in the larger world, especially the contribution of ethnicity to the richness of culture and cuisine. It would be a much impoverished world without chiles rellenos, tom kah gai, szekely goulash, pesto sauce, lamb vindaloo, coq au vin, strange-flavored beef, pasta primavera, paella, and feijoada. If we are to learn how to function well in diversified teams, we need to learn to value the diversity in skills, background, and style as much as we value diversity in diet.

Of course, I also knew a prince of a man who worked as a systems analyst with the post office and ate the same thing for lunch every day for 17 years. There are those people who just prefer to stick with the same foods all the time, and I am not sure where they fit in. A good teamwork model has room for them, but I am not sure how much they would like working on a truly diversified team — or eating at my house.

It is not always easy to tell when variety shades over into incompatibility. People often think of *The Odd Couple* as the classic case of fundamental incompatibility, yet Felix Unger and Oscar Madison really functioned quite well together considering that they perpetually drove each other crazy. In teamwork, perhaps, individual frustration may not be as important as collective performance.

Against this background must be written the growing body of disturbing evidence that programmers and computer professionals are strongly skewed in the direction of certain personality types. Australian consultant Rob Thomsett found that more than three out of five of those people in the computer field share the same basic personality profile. They are practical, logical, matter-of-fact, and realistic. They concentrate and maintain focus on useful subjects and practical issues. They are not particularly "people-oriented." Less than 20% of the general population fit this profile. This group of typical computer people also tends to perform within only certain of the team leadership roles. They are likely to be implementers, finishers, monitors, or drivers; few if any go for the coordinator or supporter styles, which are crucial for smooth and effective interpersonal functioning of a team, or for the originator role, which is essential for creative problem solving.

Thomsett blames the selection process of training and higher-level education, but there may be other factors operating here. I have management consulting colleagues in Russia who argue that computer programming represents a subculture of such power that it may have greater influence and claims to allegiance than even national culture. Their position is that programmers in Moscow are more like programmers in Minneapolis than either are like their nonprogramming compatriots from the cities in which they live and work. Whatever the causes, this trend toward uniformity may be a real handicap to our profession, especially as we work in teams.

Joshua Jacobson, conductor of Boston's Zamir Chorale and also one of my favorite philosophers, put it this way at one of our rehearsals. If everyone sings the same note, you do not get harmony. For harmony you need people singing different notes that fit together. In this he echoes another of my favorites, Heraclitus, The Obscure. He was called The Obscure not because he is any more difficult to understand than the next Greek philosopher, but because so little is known of him except indirectly and by attribution. This may account for why he is credited with so many wise and wonderful insights that seem to support such varied positions. Supposedly he said, "Εχ των διαφερ—οντων χαλλιστη αρμονια." Loosely translated from the Greek, this says, "From differing songs arises the highest harmony."

Amen, Heraclitus! Selah, Jacobson!

10

Coding Cowboys
and Software Sages[*]

Quality has become a watchword of the hour in software development. Some of the concern with quality is genuine, and some is merely panicky chief executives lunging after the bandwagon rolling by; some "quality programs" will make a difference, and some will only make for good public relations. As issues of software quality come to the fore, matters of maturity will loom larger, because an effective commitment to quality requires maturity from organizations and individuals.

Managers of software development face many new challenges as software systems become larger and more complex. Organizations are moving toward greater "process maturity" using more disciplined and sophisticated models of software development. The question in the minds of many managers is whether development professionals will live up to their name and mature with the methods. Programmers, analysts, and designers are often a breed unto themselves, and managing an entire herd of such mavericks can tax the resources of even the best managers. The problems of dealing with diehard independents who would rather quit than collaborate are major issues facing software development groups today.

Even with the surplus of loners in the field, most software is produced by groups of people working together. Some of it is produced by groups of

* Revised from *American Programmer*, July 1993.

people working separately. Some is even produced by groups of people working against each other. Very little software is developed by individuals working alone.

This obvious, simple, and seemingly inconsequential fact would not be worth stating were it not for the way in which the field of software development is dominated by myths of giants, by a mythology that glorifies the brilliant genius who single-handedly conceives and codes clever new systems in sweaty and sleepless weekends of nonstop programming. We are blessed and cursed by the promethean images of these nerdy pioneers bringing us new languages, new tools, and new paradigms for computer applications. And we are blessed and cursed by a larger cadre of lesser godlings, programmers of more limited talent but nevertheless indomitable spirit, determined individualists who insist on doing things their way, alone, without interference, without help, without the hindrances of supervision, methodology, or discussion.

Management and organizational consultants often refer to such people as "cowboys." Cowboys, the last of the rugged and untamed, are found in various fields, but nowadays many of them are punching assembly language cattle on the silicon frontier. They have also been called "human cougars," for their solitary and sometimes wary ways. They are the mavericks who either go it their own way or not at all.

In case there are any doubts, it is important to make clear that I am a maverick myself, or so I have been told. In fact, I have been officially branded a maverick by methodologist-become-historian Paul Ward in his history of structured analysis (Ward 1992). He has personally assured me that it is to be taken as a compliment. I certainly have been a nonconformist most of my professional life. Modern software engineering may have embraced many of the basic principles of structured design, with CASE tools and integrated development environments enshrining data flow diagrams and structure charts as the technical iconography of development orthodoxy, but such was not always the case. Difficult though it may be to believe, these were once the unorthodox, even radical ravings of a maverick.

I believe in mavericks; many of my best friends are mavericks. And I believe in the maverick imagination, in individual creativity as the well-spring of nearly all genuine innovation. I also recognize it as the well-spring of much monumental lunacy. For every Einstein there are a gaggle of Velikovskys. Sometimes the innovation and idiocy even spout from the same font, as from a Tesla or a Wilhelm Reich. One way or another, mavericks have enriched our lives, if not always by invention then by entertainment.

Being a cowboy is not the same as being independent or an individualist. The definition does not hinge on whether or not someone uses a particular software methodology or even any methodology at all. Being a cowboy is a frame of mind and a style of life. Cowboy coders are simply those oppositional developers who can't abide being fenced in by standards, constraints, or discipline, who resist all efforts at being reined in by supervision or collaboration with others, who put idiosyncratic originality above usability or reliability.

Of course, not every programmer who prefers to work alone is a coding cowboy. Some people are loners by temperament. Some are perhaps better described as hermits, others just prefer their own company, and many simply find the company of others distracting or even overwhelming. Some of my best work has been done with no one in the room but me and my trusty computer.

Managing Mavericks

Why is it important to manage mavericks? Why not merely turn them loose, let them join their cowboy companions as contract programmers and independent consultants? For one thing, there are so many of them. For another, a lot of them are good, and potentially could be a heck of a lot better if their creative contrariness could be tempered by a little more cooperation. Mavericks and coding cowboys have a real contribution to make to software development. Good management creates a context for capturing and utilizing this contribution for the benefit of both the organization and the cowboys.

Some managers advocate a laissez faire approach to coding cowboys. Expecting discipline or imposing standards just keeps programmers from reaching their full potential as brilliant programming cowboys.

I think managers have better options — at least I hope so. The free-rein approach probably accounts for a lot of the poor performance and unreliability of the products being shipped by many such major software companies. It shows also in the user interfaces of major software products that suffer from creeping featurism and are covered with a hodge-podge of unreconciled hooks and handles contributed by each and every member of the old programming posse.

As the size and complexity of software products grows, it is more important for project managers to learn how to use the isolated developer wisely. Even where the dominant project model is collaborative teamwork, the best managers will find ways to accommodate the needs of loners. It may not be possible to allow them to work in complete isolation, but it also may not be necessary to make them attend every meeting or code walkthrough.

Loners can do good work and they can do poor work. It is up to the manager to find ways to utilize them so that they do good work. Part of the trick is in how the work is broken down and assigned. Those who work best in isolation need to be given tasks that are more or less separable, portions of the system that can be defined as black boxes with simple interfaces and well-defined external specifications. They need to work on components that are only weakly coupled with other parts of the system, that do not require close coordination or frequent communication with others.

Another part of the trick is careful monitoring and review. Limiting the interdependencies between independents and the rest of the development team does not mean ignoring them. In fact, when part of a system is developed separately, it is even more important to monitor the interfaces and interconnections that remain. Managers often understand this when working with outside contractors or telecommuters who work at home, but tend to forget it when dealing with the independent who sits in the office down the hall.

When work is done openly in groups, increased visibility tends to reduce defects and increase quality (See Chapters 22 and 27). Work completed in some degree of isolation from a development group therefore warrants greater scrutiny in terms of conformance to external specifications and closer inspection in terms of implementation quality. It is not enough that the code works as far as acceptance testing can verify; quality assurance must also study the code itself for conformity to standards of clarity and reliability.

Mavericks and Methods

Working alone does not imply working without discipline or without good methodology, any more than working in a group guarantees results. Working in a group only guarantees there are more people involved. From the manager's perspective, however, using systematic development methodology assumes greater importance when there are developers working in isolation. Regression testing and implementation walkthroughs can only do so much in assuring quality. True quality cannot be achieved after the fact; it has to be designed and built in from the beginning. Systematic and formal methods for software development are proven ways of building in quality. The work of even the most independent coding cowboy will probably be improved and can certainly be trusted more if a systematic methodology is used.

In order to get the coding cowboys to use systematic development methods, management may have to compromise on *which* method is used. It is better that independent operators use their own idiosyncratic methods than no methods at all.

Design models not only can speed development and improve quality but can also aid traceability by providing a partial record of a developer's thought processes, an audit trail of the derivation of problems and solutions. Requiring appropriate design documents — data flow diagrams, structure charts, structured flow charts, and the like — needs to be part of the specifications for subsystems that are to be developed independently.

Project managers may find analogies to the cattle range useful to help keep in mind an assortment of approaches for dealing with programming mavericks. Trail bosses had to ride herd on their charges, watching for strays that separated themselves too far from the group, gathering them in periodically. They kept close watch on their cowhands and the cattle they herded. They also left room for cowboys to let off steam on Saturday nights.

Cowboy Collectives

Meilir Page-Jones has developed a very practical schema for understanding the ages of software process maturity. Some groups operate in the *age of anarchy*, developing software without the benefit of any systematic approaches or even codified wisdom. Everything rests on the skill of the individual. The *age of folklore* is characterized by a culture of collective wisdom, accumulated knowledge that is often embodied in stories about successes and failures or rules of thumb extracted from past experiences. The *age of methods* is based in systematic, although not necessarily formal, approaches to software development that go beyond folklore. The *age of metrics* is based on measures for evaluating quality and productivity and organized feedback for improving the development process based on measurement. Finally, we reach the *age of engineering,* in which software development becomes a true engineering discipline, a process under continuous improvement using methods that are not based in folklore or armchair speculation but on theory validated through study and research, in which design decisions and trade-offs are systematic and derived from models and metrics that embody the results of a growing body of knowledge.

Engineering is what you get when mature individuals in mature organizations use mature methods. Anarchy is what you get when you simply throw a group of coding cowboys into the corral together and point them at a problem.

Unfortunately, when mavericks are put into groups they are prone to becoming oppositional. It is not uncommon for them to end up working at cross purposes. Without creative leadership, a whole group of coding cowboys is apt to lead to unmanageable chaos.

When teamed with other less contrary types, coding cowboys can have a tendency to undermine teamwork. Some may hold back and refuse to participate in group problem solving, others may take up most of the air time with their own favorite topics and approaches. Often they are critical of any ideas they did not generate and end up in conflict with the rest of the group.

In the worst cases, the contrarions end up being pushed into a corner and scapegoated for their negative attitudes. In turn, coding cowboys may come to view the rest of a team as a bunch of groupthink bozos who couldn't code their way out of a cardboard box and don't appreciate true genius when they see it.

Managers need to know how to head off such polarization for the sake of the team and the end product. Direct confrontation may not be the preferred style of management for handling coding cowboys. It can be risky to face down cowboys. They have deserved reputations for strong opinions, sensitive egos, and itchy trigger fingers. Managers are unlikely to be able to win such a face off and may only antagonize their cowboys into even more entrenched opposition.

The real challenge facing managers is what to do about the mavericks and strays. Some would argue that they need to be cut out of the herd and put out to pasture, but this option is not always available and may not serve the best interests of the organization. My boss says that the job of the manager is to get rid of the obstacles that keep others from doing their jobs well and from fulfilling their greatest potential. Lucky me. Part of the potential of well-managed mavericks is to bring their creative energy and critical abilities to the organization.

Some kinds of teams thrive on opposition, others cannot abide dissent. It depends on the basic model by which a team is organized (Constantine 1993c; Larson and LaFasto 1989). Project teams that are based on top-down management and work assignment, that rely on traditional authority for direction, or that are headed by highly directive leaders, will have greater problems with mavericks and coding cowboys. The work of such traditional tactical teams (see Chapter 11) can be hampered by opposition, and their controlled style of organization can push mavericks into rebellion.

A free-wheeling "breakthrough" team (Chapter 12), on the other hand, can be energized by mavericks, whose independent spirit and creative individuality are just what the group needs. The issue here is how to foster creativity rather than chaos. The key to getting useful work out of such a team is promoting high levels of mutual regard and respect for each other's competence. Teams where members see their teammates as skilled professionals with good ideas can engage in healthy competition without degenerating into a free-for-all.

Teams that work by building technical consensus (see Part I) can also be good settings for mavericks. A technical consensus is one in which the contributions of all team members are taken into account in arriving at a common decision that all members feel they can support, even if they do not necessarily agree on every detail.

Opposition or criticism should never be confused with disloyalty. In fact, critical feedback is often the most valuable information and the most important to hear. Healthy skepticism and critical perspectives should be encouraged, not disparaged. The quality of group problem solving has been shown to be critically dependent on this kind of "negative feedback." Groups that include a "resident critic" or "devil's advocate," or that exploit dialectical processes of opposing ideas and active critique, perform better (Constantine 1989; Priem and Price 1991).

Managers should remember that, just as authority tries to control opposition, opposition resists control and authority. So, instead of controlling, co-opt! One way to co-opt opposition and turn it to the advantage of the team is to institutionalize it. In one approach (Constantine 1989, 1991a), the critic or "devil's advocate" is regarded as a valued contributor whose role in the group is critical to success. Like the "grit in the oyster," critical monitoring of the work of the team is the necessary irritant that forms the basis for producing programming pearls (Thomsett 1990). As a team member, the maverick is formally charged with the responsibility to critique decisions, take alternative viewpoints, note exceptions, problems, and limitations, and make sure that the group considers alternatives and explores difficulties with proposed solutions.

Mavericks are often better at criticizing than being criticized. When they go off on their own, however, their work needs to be checked and reviewed, which they may resent as intrusive and distrusting. If critical feedback to the coding cowboy is needed, it is best rendered as impersonal as possible, appealing to the analytical and critical skills of mavericks, challenging them to be creative in solving whatever problems are uncovered.

It is not surprising that the biggest limitations on mavericks are self-imposed. They can get stuck in the need to be unique, to do things differently, even at the expense of practicality. Working alone also limits the size of what they can tackle. Mavericks can end up alienating coworkers.

Dissent and Diversity

We now know that diversity in teams promotes better problem solving and decision making. Several decades of research on group dynamics has demonstrated that heterogeneity beats homogeneity almost all the time. Teams of men and women solve problems better than single-sex teams. Groups that include varied specialties and training fare better. Diversity wins, whether it is diversity in personality, in interpersonal style, or in culture or ethnic background.

Clearly, then, we do not want to get rid of all the mavericks. We want teams in which a variety of leadership styles and responses to leadership are displayed — including resistance to leadership. We need movers and shakers on our teams, innovators who will generate ideas, and champions who will drive them forward. But we also need critics and skeptics who counter unbridled enthusiasm with cool doubt, who keep uncritical support from running away with unproved notions. Opposition to leadership can even serve the team by keeping leadership within bounds.

We are hampered in exploiting opposition by simplistic notions of teamwork that are based on ideals of perfect harmony and fantasies of cooperation without conflict. For the best collective performance, contention may be the most essential ingredient in a creative process that results in a quality product.

And what is a software sage? A software sage is someone who recognizes opposition as opportunity, and who sees flexibility in frustration. A software sage is the wise old ranch hand who has been through the range wars, has been there out on the lone prairie, and has returned to the homestead. A software sage may even be a reformed cowboy or cowgirl, one who has never lost respect for the individual but who has come to value cooperation.

III

Work Organization

Introduction

Although I started out in the computer field armed with a management degree from M.I.T., I was initially more interested in the technical side of programming. It was through my work on family systems that I first became seriously involved in issues of teamwork organization and organization development. Although my career in computers and software spans more than thirty years, I took a detour of some dozen years in the middle. I was lucky then to be an applied systems theorist moving into the family field at a time when family sociology and family therapy were moving toward systems theory (Whitchurch and Constantine 1992). Marriage and family studies, sociology, and social psychology had all begun to understand how groups of people function as systems and to apply general systems theory and systems thinking to making sense of human systems.

I had the very great fortune to study and work under psychologist David Kantor, one of the cleverest investigators and most creative thinkers in the field. Kantor had been studying families by direct observation, documenting and describing the delicate dance of daily living by which families coordinate and sustain their activities and relationships. Out of his extraordinarily rich observations came the recognition that even untroubled families were not all alike. He developed a framework for understanding the varied and quite distinct models under which families functioned. His book, *Inside the Family* (Kantor and Lehr 1975), one of the most inventive works of modern social science research, has become an influential classic.

David is a better researcher, but I think I am a better theorist, so I took up the challenge of refining and filling in some of the holes in his theoretical thinking. The result was an extension of the framework to cover the full array of human systems, from families to informal groups, from project teams to multinational organizations. Eventually, my own book on "family paradigms" (Constantine 1986) was completed, and to my surprise and delight it began to be used in graduate courses in management and organization development. Eventually a loose network of management consultants around the world developed around the application of David's and my work to the world of work. It was some of these who helped convince me there were exciting things going on in the computer field and that I ought to come back, bringing along what I'd learned from studying and working with families.

11

Traditional Tactics*

Okay, people, time to get organized! The question is: how? If you work alone, you can work any darned way you please. You don't need to coordinate what you are doing with what anyone else is doing, and you don't have to get along with anyone. You can keep everything in its exact, obsessive-compulsive place and do things in the precise sequence of a standard software development life cycle model. Or you can leave everything spread out all over the office in utter chaos and code things as you get inspired or happen to think of them. However, once you have two or more people working together, the operant word is "together." The work they do and how they do it have to be coordinated.

This chapter begins an exploration of the organization and management of human work: how work is organized and how people who work together coordinate their activities (Constantine 1990a, 1991c, 1993c). Think of organization as the human equivalent of software architecture — with management corresponding to the dynamic control of program components. It's the old structure and dynamics thing again. Whether you are trying to organize a

* From *Software Development,* Volume 1, #3, March 1993.

new software company or the next programming project, many of the same issues apply.

So how do you do it? How do you get a group of people — a project team or an entire corporation — to work together? How do you organize the group, structure the work, and manage the activity? What's the right way? Here it's time for one of those standard "consultant's answers": it depends! Looking for the *right* way to organize projects is like looking for the *right* way to code a subroutine. It depends on what you are trying to accomplish (Constantine 1993c).

The bread-and-butter work of producing yet another set of print drivers or another variant on a conventional screen generator may require a very different model for organization and management than what is needed for a team devising a breakthrough CASE tool to support concurrent software engineering and consensus design of object-oriented software. In an excellent little book on teamwork, Larson and LaFasto (1989) identified several major variants on project teamwork, each of which is better at some things than others. Here we'll look at four distinct and very different models for project teamwork organization, each having advantages in certain areas and each having its own particular weaknesses.

Getting Organized

So, let's get organized! The simplest and safest way to go is the tried and true of standard operating procedure. The traditional way to coordinate the work of more than one person is to put someone in charge, making them a supervisor. The function of the supervisor is to direct and oversee the work of others. This structure can be extended by recursion. The result is a hierarchy of managers in charge of others who manage still others. This is a simple, stable, and familiar form of organization: a traditional pyramid based on a hierarchy of authority. On software projects organized along this model, the hierarchy may not be many layers deep, but it is still a hierarchy. In principle, it can be amazingly efficient; in practice it can grow into a towering bureaucracy incapable of anything but sustaining its own bureaucratic inefficiency

Such a model is more than merely a way of working; it can be a way of life. I was recently reorganizing my record collection to make room for the steadily multiplying CDs when I found a real treasure, a vintage recording of "Paean," selections from the IBM corporate songbook.* Listening to the Association of

---

* Released as a joke for one of the major computer conferences but not without its valid insight into corporate culture and politics.

British Secretaries in America (indeed!) sing their stirring rendition of "The IBM Country Club Song," I started thinking about company culture and how the way we work shapes the way we view the world as much as the other way around.

The traditional view from the pyramid sees organization as the foundation of stable performance and sees control as the key to keeping it all together. Leadership depends on authority. Managers make decisions and subordinates are expected to implement them, to show loyalty, and to accept direction from their superiors. Predictable, reliable performance is achieved through standards and procedures, through rules of operation. Everyone has their job, their role, their responsibilities, their place in the hierarchy. Corporate or divisional or project interests come first and foremost; individuals are rewarded for faithfully carrying out their part of the larger job.

In basic form, this model is really very simple. Put somebody in charge who can start making decisions and giving orders, preferably someone who knows the ropes and has come up through the business. Decision making in traditional hierarchies is supposed to be strictly top down. It may take time for a given matter to reach the right person in charge, but once it does, decision making can be quite efficient. As fast as the leader can make up her or his mind, the decision is made. No one needs to be consulted; there is no need for discussion, debate, or exploration. Obviously, this can be a strength and a weakness. It means that a lot hinges on the one at the top. Bad decisions can be made as quickly as good ones, and a leader who is too slow or out of touch can bring the entire pyramid crumbling down in ruin.

Pyramid Power

When it comes to software projects and project teamwork, the traditional model is best at what can be called tactical work. In tactical projects, the territory is familiar and the parameters are known. The most important thing is to get the work out the door. I cut my programming teeth on tactical projects, producing routine business system applications, such as payroll, cost accounting, and personnel file maintenance. Once you have done a couple of payroll systems, they all begin to look alike. Even if they really aren't, seeing them that way helps you to simplify, making it easier to build and maintain standard ways of doing things. Eventually, you know all the steps and can do them in your sleep.

Clarity is the make-or-break issue for tactical teamwork — clear requirements, clear directions, clear roles. Within this world, development methods are more effective when they are well defined, with clear standards and guidelines. A detailed software development life cycle is specified within which successive phases are carried out. Work is expected to be accurate and efficient. The focus of the group in such a team is on the task at hand. Period. What team members need most is clear direction from project leaders and management. Team members are assigned specific portions of the well-understood work and do what they are supposed to do.

Traditional hierarchy works. Many companies in our industry and countless software projects have been organized along these lines, including some of the biggest success stories in computing. Corporate songbooks extolling fearless leaders and loyal followers are the artifacts of some of the largest and best examples.

Such a well-defined and predictable environment can be comforting, but not everyone is comfortable fitting into that world. Those who do are likely to be loyal, committed, and action-oriented. They attach a sense of importance to the work they are doing more than to themselves, and they respond well to directions from leaders. They probably prefer to pay more attention to programs than people. Tactical teams are havens for conformists and obsessive-compulsives, for salt-of-the-earth basic programmers. Tactical teams work well for those who want to know what to do and just do it.

On the downside, any group organized as a traditional hierarchy can somewhat too easily get stuck in a rut, resisting useful innovation in the interests of maintaining stable authority, and ultimately spending more energy on rigidly enforcing standards and procedures than on solving problems or producing products. At their best, they are efficient and productive but not very innovative. To the extent that they do innovate, it is likely to be incremental improvements on established technology, evolution rather than revolution. Looking at the large industry leaders who rely on traditional hierarchy, we often find that their major innovations have come from acquisitions or from small internal spin-offs.

Companies and software groups organized along these lines are likely to have particular difficulty dealing with cowboy coders (Chapters 7, 8, and 10). Independent individualists and traditional hierarchy are an immiscible combination. Those who resist or question authority, who insist on going their own way or departing from standards, are likely to find themselves passed over for raises or on the short list for downsizing.

From the top of the pyramid or buried somewhere within, it may look like there is no other way to organize and manage. After all, somebody has to be in charge, right? Either you lead, you follow, or you get out of the way. Some people still don't see any alternative to hierarchy for human organizations. But then we once thought that nested subroutines topped by a control executive were the only way to modularize programs. Now we have communities of communicating objects and peer-to-peer networks with distributed databases.

And people are ever so much more flexible than programs. At least *some* people.

12

Chaos Manners[*]

I have some good news for all the coding "cowboys" and "cowgirls" out there. There is a kind of organization that not only tolerates but depends for its vitality on utilizing the talents of true independents.

It may come as a shock to some old-timers or young hard-liners, but neither hierarchy nor authority are necessary for groups of people to work together effectively. Indeed, a worldwide management revolution may be taking place, as more and more companies in numerous industries discover the advantages of self-directed teams, autonomous work groups, and managing without managers. One of the big problems with the traditional management pyramid is that it is so dense in the middle — in more than one sense of the phrase. All those layers of middle management cost, not only in terms of dollars but also in terms of responsiveness. The closer you try to dance along the precipitous leading edge of any technology, the more unwieldy the pyramid becomes. Genuine innovation requires an agility beyond the traditional tactics of top-down management.

Breaking Through

For real breakthroughs that push technology beyond the edge into unexplored regions, project teams are more likely to succeed by turning to the flexibility of independent action and the full force of individual creativity, unhampered by command-and-control. The trick is to bring out and capitalize on the inventive

[*] From *Software Development*, Volume 1, #5, May 1993

energy of independent thinkers, encouraging free exploration and individual initiative, to foster a kind of creative chaos that hovers on the supercharged edge of running completely amok, a sort of controlled insanity that breaks out of accepted modes of thinking and challenges assumptions about limits and possibilities. All these things run absolutely counter to the closed patterns of corporate pyramid power because they undermine authority and throw tradition to the winds — profoundly threatening to the traditional management mentality, but precisely what is needed to break new ground.

The key ingredients for a breakthrough initiative are, in fact, the exact antithesis of the tradition-bound hierarchical model. Instead of putting stability ahead of change, instability is promoted, becoming the driving force to overcome blindly accepted practices and unquestioned notions. Instead of putting corporate and collective interests above individual ones, individual freedom of expression and action come first. Where the traditional pyramid tries to rein in cantankerous coding "cowboys" and "cowgirls," breakthrough teams love them and let them run free. This free-wheeling atmosphere stimulates creativity and tends to promote the "personal best" performances that can generate breakthroughs.

Breakthrough teams actually depend on individual initiative to coordinate their activities. Decisions are not centralized but are made independently, close to the action, by whomever encounters the problems and has the know-how to resolve them. What keeps such a group on course is a kind of friendly competition; what keeps them from running off in every direction at once is their common interest in and love of the game and their mutual respect for each other as players.

You are most likely to find this model operating in smaller high-tech companies, entrepreneurial start-ups, and the research and development divisions of larger organizations. They can be remarkably successful. Indeed, many a muscle-bound corporate behemoth relies on an undisciplined "corporate skunkworks" for the new ideas and products that keep the collective engine primed and running.

Work and Play

Consider this scenario in an archetypal Pacific coast company drawn from real experience. You enter the lobby to find the phones being handled by a bearded, middle-aged guy who turns out to be the veep for R&D. You tell him you are a GUI consultant and he waves you down the hall to the left. Ducking a barely subsonic frisbee that sails past, you try to find someone in charge. No luck.

Recognizing a screen on a workstation in one office, you approach someone who is browsing through a familiar class library and turns out to be the receptionist. But conversation becomes increasingly difficult as the pace of the hallway frisbee game picks up. A couple of programmers, who are busy debugging work-arounds to an operating system problem, holler for quiet but end up getting drawn into the melee of flying discs. Soon the entire department has adjourned to the adjacent parking lot for a furious five-frisbee tournament.

To a casual observer, it may look like bedlam or kindergarten, but during this particular frisbee game a couple of programmers get inspired by the pattern in which the group keeps multiple frisbees flying without interference. They devise from it a novel solution to a nagging problem in the groupware that the department has been developing. Was it dumb luck? Were they just fooling around on the job? Impossible to tell in such a group. Work is play and play is work. Is the receptionist a software engineer? You never know.

And what about the V.P. of R&D, is he part of the support staff? He is if he's any good. Effective managers of this kind of creative chaos know that their real job is to provide resources and support, run interference for the group, and stay out of the way. The best such managers and team leaders are also likely to be techies themselves, basically one of the bunch, but particularly respected for their own programming prowess or other technical talents.

Of course, it doesn't always work, and even when it is working, inventive nuttiness can have its downside. It can be darned difficult holding a planning meeting or a code walkthrough when staff are always coming and going and those in the room may be preparing e-mail on a laptop or playing chess on a pocket board. And communications within a breakthrough team can be haphazard at best, even when everyone is in the same room. Not that these creative independents are uncommunicative, just that information can too easily get lost in the chaos. ("Oh, yeah, the client did message us last week about a change in the interface protocol. The note got filed someplace. I think.")

The brilliant and decidedly independent psychologist David Kantor was among the first to observe that apparent randomness in human groups disguises an underlying, complexly patterned logic (Kantor and Lehr 1975). In this, his studies anticipated more recent work applying chaos theory to groups. Kantor recognized two variants of apparent randomness, one he called creative and the other chaotic, in the older and more traditional sense of chaos. The difference between "random creative" and "random chaotic" is crucial; it is the difference between success and failure in achieving a software breakthrough.

In extreme cases, a breakthrough team can become a *breakdown* team. Without the right ingredients, friendly competition can become unfriendly, unproductive, and even desperate. Would-be contributors work at cross purposes and fight for resources. Eventually, people may spin completely out of control, leaving the organization and project in shambles.

The first necessary ingredient to avoid chaotic collapse is good people, bolstered by good training and tools. Members of the team must have skills and abilities that are up to the challenge of the project and that are recognized by other members of the team. Mutual respect for technical competence and an implicit trust in the ability of other members to contribute to the effort are the essential glue holding the breakthrough team together.

The second necessary ingredient for success is sufficient, even abundant resources. The almost brownian motion of whole teams of innovators can lead to extraordinary solutions, but not typically with the greatest efficiency. New algorithms have to be tried out, novel data structures have to be implemented, and clever screen layouts have to be prototyped. The process of freely creating and trying out alternative ideas is essential; even dead ends that have to be abandoned are often an important part of the group learning process. Creativity comes at a cost and requires risk taking.

Opposing Charges

How do you lead a bunch of inventive independents? Not by taking charge. Leadership of breakthrough teams is a rather special role, radically different from management in traditional tactical teams. The most effective team and project leaders are peers who are highly respected as programmers and problem solvers, who are charismatic trend-setters to whom others naturally look. They lead by example rather than edict — which would almost certainly be resisted — and are able to foster an atmosphere of high mutual regard among team members. They are also good at getting needed resources — work stations, software, training, more time — for the team, keeping it well fueled and heading off any potential breakdown into counterproductive competition for scarce resources.

For success, breakthrough teams also need autonomy: freedom from interference, freedom to explore unanticipated angles and approaches. Good leaders of such teams say, "Let the games begin!" then stay out of the way. The best ones also make sure that nobody else gets in the way either.

A project team organized and managed for creative breakthrough can be a fun, interesting environment in which to work, but not everyone can work well in such a setting. People who need clear directions, well-defined goals, and straightforward expectations are likely to be more comfortable in a traditional hierarchy. The kinds of developers who perform best in breakthrough teams may be either artistic or intellectual, but they are sure to be seen as independent-minded. They are self-starters who don't wait for directions, but more than that, the best performers are also perversely persevering. Good tactical team members are often those who are especially responsive to direction from leaders, but good innovators are likely to be more individualistic, even resistant to authority and direction.

It probably would make little sense to turn an entire cadre of creative cowboys and cowgirls loose on a routine database application for the accounting department; the poor accountants might themselves be driven to stampede. On the other end of the scale, massive projects marked by countless components and complex interdependencies — the civilian space station software, for instance — are not the bailiwick of breakthrough teams, even when there is a clearly recognizable need for innovation. Teams of creative independents, for obvious reasons, fit better with smaller and simpler projects that do not require close coordination of too many highly interdependent parts.

The large-scale complexity of many modern software projects is better approached by other project models to be discussed in later chapters. In the meantime, the Nanomush Corporation and International Behemoth Management, Inc., types will have to continue to muddle their way through with their chaotic cowpokes and their megapyramids.

13

Open Architects*

Many folks believe that there are basically two kinds of people. The rest of us, of course, are different; we know better. So it is when it comes to work and organizations. There are those who think the choice is between orderly authority and unbridled anarchy — or between freedom and oppression — and that's it! The rest of us know it is never that simple. Whatever managers and management consultants may do to simplify the story, real people in real organizations defy the limitations of simple dichotomies and slip out of the one-dimensional conceptual boxes into which we try to stuff them.

On the one hand, we have the hierarchical model for work organization discussed in Chapter 11 and on the other, its exact opposite, the creative anarchy explored in Chapter 12. And in between the extremes of ordered traditionalism and freestyle innovation are scattered as many variations as there are projects and people to work on them.

Not every working group falls somewhere along this line, however. Some, quite far off in left field, do not see the basic issues of work organization as trade-offs. These are the people who think "both/and" rather than "either/or," who say, "We can work it out." Both traditionalists and their free-spirited competition tend to see an essential tension between "me" and "we." In the traditional hierarchy, the interests of individuals are subordinated to those of the team or group or organization; in innovative individualism, the individual reigns supreme and collective interests are moved backstage.

---

* From *Software Development*, Volume 1, #6, June 1993

Others, however, believe there is no essential conflict between the whole and its parts, just as there is no need to choose between change and stability. Their approach to working together, officially known as the "open paradigm," is a model for flexibility based on egalitarian cooperation and communication. In descriptive shorthand, we could call this model "adaptive collaboration," an open-ended architecture for human organization.

Hanging Loose, Hanging Together

Adaptive collaboration is tailored for technical problem solving. It values neither tradition and stability nor innovation and change in themselves. What is important in this view of projects and progress is the adaptive fit between how the team is working and what it is they are working on. Today we're designing independent programs, so we work separately; tomorrow we have to come up with a common communications protocol, so we meet as a group; everyone has something to say about database architecture, so let's get all the ideas out on the table.

The aim in such a group is to hang loose and talk things through so that competing goals can be integrated and alternative approaches can be synthesized. They are, in a sense, continually reinventing themselves, changing the way they work to fit the needs of the moment and the group's long-term goals. Who is "in charge" and how they are in charge depends on what the group is doing.

Development groups organized along these lines tend to be more of a flat circle than a pyramid. Team members work as colleagues with interchangeable roles. Unlike the free radicals of "breakthrough" teams, who may work quite independently and even competitively, these colleagues closely coordinate their efforts. Decisions are made collectively, through discussions, negotiation, and consensus building. This does not mean that everyone agrees on everything, but that they work on the basis of a technical consensus. A technical consensus is one in which all team members can support the group's actions and choices on all essential matters. This requires getting everyone's input on matters of importance. Technical consensus assures that co-workers "buy in" to the joint effort and feel pride of personal ownership in the collective product.

Because they talk things through together, these groups really shine on solving complex problems, especially where substantial quantities of information have to be exchanged and examined (which sounds suspiciously like a lot of software development). In fact, the more factors and facets and widgets and whatsits to the problem, the greater the relative advantage of open teams over tactical teams, where information may be too tightly controlled, and breakthrough teams, where information can get lost in the competition and chaos.

Breakthrough groups, putting a premium on free-thinking originality, may also come up with brilliant innovations that fall short of being completely practical. Their stolid counterparts in tactical teams may produce dependably routine programs but miss out on more creative possibilities in data structures or algorithms or user interfaces. Collaborative problem-solving teams are in the best position to pull together disparate ideas from all their members to produce solutions that are both practical and innovative.

Real collaboration requires the right kind of leadership, leadership that encourages free discussion and helps to build technical consensus. The best managers for open problem-solving projects tend to be working colleagues, competent professionals themselves who play an active technical role in analysis, design, and construction. Typically, they do not lead meetings or technical discussions themselves, because they don't want to bias the outcome. Instead, they let others facilitate the discussion, drawing out the best contributions of all members. This takes a certain act of faith, a belief that the group as a whole knows more and can come up with better solutions than any one member — including the manager! Managers who are convinced that they are the smartest and best and can lay out programs better than everyone else on the project put together are not likely to fare as well as collaborative colleagues. They might do better on their own or heading a traditional tactical team.

Not surprisingly, the strong suit of adaptive collaboration can also be a handicap. These people can talk up a storm. When an hour's discussion won't resolve an issue, they're ready to spend a couple more. Not only do they haggle over the technical issues, but the philosophy behind the issues; not only do they question the development methods, but the assumptions on which they are based. Even the way the group itself operates is grist for the mill, as they examine their own methods and structures and try to adapt them to fit the problem. ("Hey, guys, maybe we need to split up into subgroups on this part of the system, work for a few days, then reconvene to try to pull it together.")

There are ways to cut down on the wheel-spinning tendencies of problem-solving teams. Decisions can be time-boxed. If a technical consensus is not reached by a specific deadline, the issue may be set aside, or defaulted to some set solution, or put into the hands of the manager for arbitration. Although each of these options somewhat violates the rules of consensual decision making, as long as they remain uncommon exceptions, the payoffs in efficiency can offset some loss in the sense of ownership in the results.

But it depends; there is no simple formula. To remain open, each group has to find its own way, negotiating its own procedures and exceptions.

Keeping the Door Open

One of the best collaborative groups I ever knew was known as the Theory Construction Workshop, an independent working group loosely affiliated with a professional society. Members met as colleagues trying to advance a common enterprise of theory construction in an atmosphere of free discussion and mutual support. Its meetings were completely open to anyone who shared an interest in building better theory. The content and format of meetings were negotiable within the group's strong tradition of enhanced cooperation and communication. Inevitably, at almost every annual business meeting, some newcomer, flush with the excitement of joining in such a rare and wonderful interchange, would propose some form of institutionalization — incorporation, membership credentials, bylaws, printed proceedings, or the like. Every year we would dutifully discuss and debate these proposals; every year they would be defeated, the consensus being to stay open, informal, and flexible.

Then one year, without thinking it through, I arose with a radical proposal. Henceforth, to avoid wasting time deliberating these perennial proposals, all attempts to institute fixed and formal rules or structures would be banned. Even before I could finish my thought, I started laughing at my own self-contradictory suggestion. Our sincere and serious consideration of even the most ill-considered suggestions from the rankest newcomer were precisely what made the group process work. Everyone smiled, I sat down, and we went back to debating the latest plan for formal proceedings. To stay open, an open process must remain open to alternatives.

Steven Sondheim ends his brilliant theater piece, *Sunday in the Park with George*, in a wonderfully open-ended way with words attributed to Georges Seurat: "White, a blank page or canvas, his favorite: so many possibilities."

My favorite, too.

14

Synchronized Swimming[*]

Want to see real rapid application development? Rent a video of the Harrison Ford movie, *Witness*, then fast forward to the scene where the Amish community builds a barn in a single day. The most remarkable thing about this particular project team is not their impressive efficiency but that there is really no leader, not even the need for leaders or leadership. They do not talk much and certainly don't have to debate over the design of the barn or negotiate who does what to build it; they just get right to work and continue to work rapidly and efficiently, in near perfect harmony, until the job is done.

This is a manager's dream come true, a kind of management utopia. "Utopia," of course, literally means "no place," and the scene from *Witness* actually happens with some regularity down in Lancaster County, Pennsylvania. "Eutopia," meaning "good place," is probably a better word. Eutopia is obviously where you want to be, an ideal. So we could call this model of project and work organization *eutopian teamwork*.

Being a software development manager in management eutopia is easy — so easy that you hardly have to lead at all. The people around you do whatever needs to be done on a software project without you looking over their shoulders or spelling things out for them. Things run so smoothly because the people who work for you and with you share your vision for the team — what you are doing and how you are going to do it. These are your kind of people; they think like you and see the world much as you do. You hardly have to say a word and they

---

[*] From *Software Development*, Volume 1, #17, July 1993.

are off designing the next set of modules or coding the GUI extensions or doing whatever else is needed. Everything fits together — the people, the software, the programming — exactly as if you had worked it all out yourself, except you didn't have to figure it out. There is no conflict on the team and no insubordination. Like a synchronized swimming team, it's the very embodiment of precise perfection and harmony.

This eutopian fantasy is the last of our four basic models of project organization: the *synchronous paradigm*, a model for eutopian teamwork. Traditional tactical teams are coordinated by hierarchical authority, breakthrough teams by individual initiative, and problem-solving teams by collaborative communication. Eutopian teams depend on alignment; team members are aligned with the direction established by a shared vision and common values. Because they all understand and are in basic agreement with this common image of where the group is going and how they are going to get there, they are able to work cooperatively with almost invisible coordination. Although it is uncommon for visionary alignment to be the dominant unifying principle of an entire organization over extended periods of time, many groups, large and small, depend on some degree of alignment or function synchronously for shorter periods.

Where Nowhere Is

An incident that happened to a colleague of mine some years ago illustrates this mode of operation. An organization development consultant was meeting with clients in a hospital conference room when one leg of a massive oak conference table buckled. The table fell on her foot, twisting her leg and trapping her. Instantly, the others sprang into action. Two lifted the heavy table from her foot while another held her hand reassuringly. Someone else called ahead to x-ray while yet another slipped into the hall to get a gurney. Not a word passed among the members of this medical team. They all knew exactly what needed to be done and each simply started doing a part of it. No one had to take charge and no discussion or negotiation was necessary, yet they were not working at cross purposes.

There is nothing magical about this kind of synchronous operation. If you watched them closely enough, you would spot the communication going on, but it is largely nonverbal and relies heavily on tacit agreement and prior knowledge. As each member of the team sees what others are doing, they adjust their own actions to fit. That way everybody doesn't go for the phone at once and the gurney is available when needed.

Provided they understand the task well enough, eutopian teams can achieve high performance under demanding or critical conditions — like the situation in the hospital conference room — or for predictable and well-understood tasks of longer duration — such as the rural barn-raising. Their image and knowledge of the task and how it is best carried out is essential. Every worker in the Amish community had seen a barn-raising and probably participated in a number of them. Everyone in the hospital conference room had extensive experience with medical emergencies. It was almost certain that none of them had ever dealt with a falling conference table before, but that was unnecessary; their experience and training as medical professionals allowed them to quickly understand this new situation in a common way.

The key to effectiveness in eutopian teams is full commitment by all members to a sufficiently complex and well-articulated vision of the mission and methods of the group. If this alignment is weak or incomplete, or the vision itself is inadequate, the group will be unable to do the work without consultation or without conflict or will be unable to respond to the demands of changing conditions; they will either need tighter management or will run into more difficulties.

The first three of our basic team models and their underlying mechanisms are well understood by people who study management and organizations. Less is known about project teams that rely predominantly on alignment for coordination. Although purely synchronous groups may be relatively uncommon in the workplace, the combination of strong synchrony with traditional hierarchy is less rare. You are likely to find it in established companies doing business in mature industries with long traditions. Consultant Rob Thomsett and I found a number of quite synchronous software development groups within the British-modeled business of Australian banking. In Japan, where the corporate world holds conformity and uniformity in highest regard, even high-tech firms may rely heavily on synchronous alignment.

Smooth Waters

Eutopian teamwork is essentially the opposite of the collaborative model. Instead of talking and negotiation, the norm is not talking; after all, who needs to negotiate when people think so much alike that they are almost certain to agree from the start! The down side of such eutopian harmony is that under ordinary everyday operation all that peaceful cooperation can become somewhat dull. Since members of such a team get used to working with little or no discussion, they may not even communicate when they need to. When market conditions or underlying technology change radically or unexpectedly, they may not be able to respond or adapt as well as groups built on individual initiative or collaborative communication. At worst, they may continue on their contented way, oblivious to the world changing around them. If it is not a part of their shared vision, they may not see something as needing attention or response.

According to popular images, modern managers need to learn to survive in white water or to swim with the sharks and still succeed. While it is certainly possible to swim with sharks and survive, most swimmers would probably prefer warm, smooth waters. A synchronized swimming team would be well advised to stay out of white water altogether and far away from shark infested waters. Likewise, eutopian teams are better adapted to stable, consistent, and unhostile environments.

Even for teams built primarily on other models, though, a little synchrony can be useful. Closer alignment with a richer vision reduces the need for tight controls of any kind and increases the extent to which individual efforts reinforce and support rather than cancel out or interfere with each other.

Effective leaders of eutopian teams are charismatic gurus who can shape and share a sophisticated vision and draw others into committing to it. Especially important for the long haul is their ability to revise and expand this vision to fit new needs and reestablish alignment with the revision.

But, of course, I think you all know what I am talking about. You are my kind of people and we understand each other. Right? So there's no need to say anything more. (Say, this eutopian alignment is great!)

$$\boxed{15}$$

Team Politics *

The software project was an immense success. The programming team was stellar, churning out an amazing new system with enhanced features and a slick graphical interface. Then management killed the product.

No team is an island. Groups that work well as a team in the conference room may fail when it comes to the larger arena of corporate politics. Failure is failure. It's not enough to know the applications programming interface and the class library; it's not enough to know consensus and concurrent engineering processes. Unless you know how to play the game, you lose. The name of the game is "external environment."

Software teams need to manage their boundaries, protecting their territory but also building bridges. The new compiler is part of a suite of tools. The decision support system must interface with the accounting system, but it must also be used by executives to be useful for the business. A reputation as a bunch of unmanageable screw-ups can put a team on the short list for downsizing, but a rep as C++ super heroes could also lead to unreasonable expectations on the next object-oriented boondoggle launched by the president's son-in-law.

We've been looking at software teamwork in terms of models that shape internal styles of working, but Deborah Ancona at M.I.T.'s Sloan School of Management has been looking at how teams function in the larger environment of corporate realities, how their external strategies and styles affect performance

* From *Software Development*, Volume 1, #8, August 1993.

(Ancona and Caldwell 1992). She studied consulting and new product teams, as well as sales and management teams. What she has learned over the years fits with my experience with programming teams.

Through the Dimensions

The external strategies of teams are a complex matter. The team leader or project manager may play a key role in managing outside relations, but there's more to it than just your boss dealing with her boss. Teams need to manage various interfaces and interconnections with numerous parts of the organization. These interactions really take place in several dimensions: the power structure, the task structure, and the information structure.

Think of the power dimension as vertical. The important external connections in this dimension are upward. Few teams achieve real high performance without learning how to "manage up." They need "ambassadors," politicians who know how to play organizational politics and work the power structure, effectively marketing the project and the team, as well as building and maintaining a good group reputation through how they represent the team and its interests to others. Public relations can have a lot to do with team success, since a team's reputation can become a self-fulfilling prophecy. "Good" teams get the pick of projects and priority access to new software and machines. A lot of success can be a matter of taking on the doable challenges and passing on the boring and the impossible.

The most important political issue for teams is probably the need to identify and secure effective sponsorship within upper management. Well-placed sponsors or mentors can do more for a development team than all the CASE tools and work stations in Silicon Valley. Good politicians, well connected and fast on their feet, can also buffer for a software team, protecting it from the shifting winds of influence and interests as divisions are sold and companies are acquired, as middle managers move or CIOs come and go.

Task coordination is essentially a horizontal matter, involving lateral connections across functions, managing a team's working interdependence with other organizational units. Good coordinators bargain with other groups, trading services or essential resources, getting feedback on progress in other parts of the project that may have to function with the team's product. They keep the work flowing in and out of the team, making sure that component libraries are available, passing on specs to the people generating test suites, or clearing screen layouts with the human factors group.

The information dimension is also largely lateral. Liaison here involves investigating, gathering information needed for project success, sharing selected data with others. The team researchers effectively act as gatekeepers for information, screening it so that other developers don't have to wade through piles of documentation, chasing down missing pieces so that data is available when needed.

Just as teams develop distinct styles of working internally, specializing in different things, they also seem to develop characteristic ways of managing their boundaries and interacting with the rest of an organization. Among the teams that Ancona studied were four variants, which we'll call the politicians, the researchers, the isolationists, and the generalists.

Political teams specialized in "working vertically," concentrating their efforts on good relations with the higher-ups. Researcher teams were specialists in scouting out and gathering in information. Isolationist teams, on the other hand, kept themselves apart, protecting and patrolling their tightly closed boundaries. They were not very well connected in terms of power, task, or information.

The generalist teams did it all. They were well integrated into the organization through a mix of interface management activities. They were plugged into the information network through "research" and "scouting" activities, coordinated with other teams and functions through the work-flow network, and politically connected and protected in terms of the power structure.

How did these various kinds of teams fare in the real world? Team performance can be looked at from the inside or from the outside, as team members see it or as the larger organization sees it. Members of the political and the isolated teams alike thought they were the greatest, but top management saw things a little differently. In early evaluations they tended to rate the politicians and the generalists as top performers, both of these types being better tapped into the power structure.

Final Scores

A different picture emerges over the long haul. When teams were evaluated a year and a half later, the politicians had fallen from grace, earning the lowest performance ratings. Apparently these were teams that talked a good line but failed to produce. (Sounds like politicians everywhere, doesn't it?)

Researchers, who sometimes never got beyond information gathering, often ended up being disbanded by management. Isolationist teams turned out to be a mixed bag. Most of these self-contained groups failed miserably, but a few were outstanding successes. Keeping your team of crack coders insulated from the rest of the company may look like a good way to concentrate on the end product, but it could be one of those high-risk, high-payoff maneuvers.

The generalist teams, with their well-orchestrated and diversified external strategies, came out the corporate winners. Such teams seem to balance internal performance with external demands. They get the information they need but don't get stuck in perpetual research. They work the system in terms of the power structure and work flow in order to reach their goals. In other words, high-performance project teamwork is more than working well together. It's also working well with others.

So, ask not for whom the gong sounds. If you have to ask, your team has an ineffective external strategy. It sounds for thee.

16

Having It All*

No team is all things to all projects. Some teams will be better at routine development, some will excel on the most intricate applications, still others are best at breaking new ground. In part, it depends on how the team is organized and coordinated. Set up your team with fixed job assignments and run it from the top down with tight controls and close supervision and you are not likely to see much in the way of innovation. Loosely run teams that foster independent initiative are more able to chart new territory; traditional teams with fixed roles are better on well-understood applications. Teams that promote open discussion and consensus building do better on really complex problems. Depending on the nature of the problem you are facing and the technical objectives of the project, one kind of teamwork organization or another will increase your chances of success.

But you knew all that. Unfortunately, the work you do doesn't fit nicely into one of the standard boxes. Your software projects are neither without precedent nor strictly routine. The problems are complex and multifaceted, yet, to deliver on time and meet requirements, high levels of dependable development performance must be seasoned with some clever invention. You might even be tempted to give some form of creative collaboration a try, but the boss doesn't understand this touchy-feely team stuff anyway and is going to hold you and you alone accountable.

This is the way of the world, at least the world of software. None of the more or less clean teamwork models discussed in Chapters 11 through 14

* From *Software Development*, Volume 1 #9, September 1993.

quite fits the bill for the typical software project. What is needed is a more or less dirty combination tailored to the grimy details of software reality.

Management Models

Actually, real programming groups provide an abundance of messy mixtures and mongrel models, but, although some of them are more successful than others, most are either trial-and-error patchworks or are based on management models from other fields. We would like to have a project teamwork model tailored to software development, one in which the predictability of organized and established procedures and the simple accountability you get when one person is in charge are combined with the high visibility and potential for creative consensus of free-wheeling collaboration.

Coming from different points of view and working independently on different continents, Australian consultant Rob Thomsett and I both tackled this problem and designed similar solutions (Thomsett 1990; Constantine 1989, 1991a). Software teams may work best when they are carefully structured to make open collaboration and consensus engineering more efficient and manageable. This "structured open" approach combines elements of the traditional closed and collaborative open teamwork models. The team is a traditional hierarchy as viewed from outside — a single project leader is held accountable — but internally it functions as a collaborative community of peers. There are well-defined roles within the team, but these are rotated among members. There are rules and formal procedures, but these are devised to promote free exploration and consensus building. Every aspect of this approach has been designed to offset shortcomings of one model with features borrowed from the other. Nothing is fundamentally new in the Constantine-Thomsett model, but the combination is interesting in its own right.

To begin with, the project leader, who is ultimately accountable for the outcome, is expected to be an active participant in the discussions and work of the team without dominating. In particular, the project leader never leads working sessions; instead, these are led by a neutral facilitator. Open-style consensus engineering can be dramatically more efficient if discussions are facilitated by neutral discussion leaders rather than by project managers (see chapters 1 through 3). On the other hand, collaborative problem solving can too easily get bogged down in distracting side issues or fruitless debate. These are best terminated by the accountable project leader, who can set the topic aside temporarily or, on rare occasions, act as final arbiter when the group is hopelessly deadlocked.

Keeping a visible, permanent record of the twists and turns of group development work also makes the process more reliable and manageable. A structured "group memory" can keep track of decisions, rationales, work products, deferred decisions, things to do and find out, and even rejected approaches. The group memory enhances traceability and makes discussions more efficient. Key information and conclusions remain available and arguments are less likely to be forgotten and repeated. The group memory can also simplify and speed discussions by providing a convenient place to record things that become distractions or can't be resolved right away.

Both facilitators and recorders need to stay on the sidelines of technical debates if the group is to do the best job. Because typical software groups can't afford and don't have access to trained outside facilitators and recorders, these functions are turned into rotating roles instead of job descriptions. The person facilitating discussion changes with the changing course of meetings, and the structured group memory becomes the responsibility of the entire team, rotating the role of "information manager" (the "lowly and exalted scribe" of Chapter 4) among members.

Meeting Management

Structured open teams do much of their work face-to-face. This does not mean wasting time in meetings; it means working sessions, collaborating as a group on defining functionality and requirements, analyzing problems, laying out system architecture, reviewing designs, even coding critical sections. The idea is to lower defects and improve quality by increasing the visibility of work (see Chapter 22) and by taking advantage of the varied skills and perspectives that team members bring to a project.

Other functional roles may be shared by the team and rotated among members. These include maintaining access to applications expertise, especially important in object-oriented development and for user interface design, and providing liaison with the larger organization (the "team politics" discussed in the preceding chapter). Recognizing that critical feedback is an essential ingredient in improving software quality, the role of "resident critic" is formally recognized as an official part of the team. The resident critic is responsible for such things as pointing out problems and alternatives, keeping the group from closing in too quickly on an easy but inferior solution. But no team member gets to be permanent curmudgeon; it's a temporary role that is rotated. For awhile you get to be the skeptical critic, then it's my turn.

The main features of the structured open model — facilitated working sessions, structured group memory, rotating team roles — are optimized for software and applications development. By striking a creative balance between structure and flexibility, the model makes technical consensus more efficient and tactical performance more flexible.

Okay, those of you who remember your Heinlein are thinking "tan-staafl,"* and, indeed, this model has its down side, too. It takes extra training and practice to get up to speed. Not all managers are comfortable with abdicating part of their control to function as peers within a team. Formal role assignments and strict rotation can be too cumbersome for smaller teams. It's silly for one person to facilitate and another to record while the one remaining programmer engages in a lively monologue on icon design. Very small teams either have to make major compromises or use a different model.

Anyway, in the spirit of the model, I'm open to ideas for improved structure.

---

* For those who missed the classic Robert A. Heinlein novel, *The Moon is a Harsh Mistress,* "There ain't no such thing as a free lunch!"

17

Contrarion Conspiracy[*]

New England is famed for its winters and its roads. We have colorful regional habits when it comes to marking our streets and byways. For example, New England street signs typically identify only cross streets, not the main thoroughfares. After all, so the Yankee logic goes, everyone should know Main Street or Massachusetts Avenue. What would be the point of marking them? A sign on an interstate may warn you that the exit for Middleboro is coming up in one mile, but at the exit it's labeled "Sherwood and Beanville Exit." Then, at the bottom of the off ramp you are offered the choice of left to Merton or right to Chester! If you don't know where to turn, perhaps you have no business being there. I am convinced this logic is also followed by certain software developers, who use one term in the manual, another in the on-line help, and an unrelated icon on the button bar. Navigating their menus and dialogue boxes is like getting to Freeport from West Roxbury via Providence. As they say Down East, "You can't get there from here."

Some of our expressway interchanges are works of art. We don't quite have the traffic volume of, say, an LA, but we make up for it with the most convoluted highway interchanges in the world. These asphalt pretzels are capable of turning even light traffic into a snarl. A few cars with out-of-state license plates or one stalled vehicle anytime after three on a weekday and it's parking lot city.

* From *Software Development*, Volume 1, #4, April 1993.

The most mind-boggling of the elaborate interchanges in the Greater Boston area were, I have become convinced, designed by specialized contractors. Such monuments to creative complexification require engineering genius and a commitment to perversity. For example, a westbound vehicle leaving a toll road for a northbound alternate might have to make a left exit, crossing under the eastbound traffic, then enter rotary traffic for three-quarters of the circle, bear right, stop for tolls, next cross under both original eastbound and westbound lanes, then over entering street-level traffic, then onto the northbound on-ramp, merging with another on-ramp for one-half mile before finally squeezing left into traffic. Got that? Remind you of a favorite Windows program?

The best of Massachusetts's macadam monstrosities could never have been developed by any conventional notion of teamwork. Traditional teams are incapable of such heights of multileveled mania. No, these require a model of project organization that must certainly have counterparts in software development. They must have been designed and built by a group modeled on a fundamentally different paradigm: the Contrarion Conspiracy!

The Contrarion Conspiracy is an international cabal of engineers, technicians, and managers in numerous fields. Their secret icon is the Knot of Gordius, their avowed purpose, the ultimate complexification of everything. They are guided by the Contrarion Credo: Different or dead. What matters is not that a system be usable or even reasonable, only that it be different, that it have more doodads. Look-and-feel *über alles*.

Use It or Lose It

The ghost of Cyril Northcote Parkinson is the god of the conspiracy. Their most sacred operating principle is to let no resource go unused. For every off-ramp there must be an overpass. For every obscure API call there must be a use, and a truly good program uses them all. A system that does not ship compressed on at least ten high-density disks or, better yet, CD-ROM, can hardly be worth what you paid for it. The installed footprint must be at least 25 megabytes. Installation should create numerous new directories, at least some of which are subdirectories to \WINDOWS, into which various obscurely named files will also be plunked along with the new product's own.INI files. And, of course, installation can hardly be said to be robust unless WIN.INI, CONFIG.SYS, AUTOEXEC.BAT, and even SYSTEM.INI are extensively doctored. Otherwise some unhappy user might be able to remove the software just by deleting a few files and directories.

The Contrarion Conspiracy has roots in civil engineering and municipal contracting, where the name of the game is to use as much brick and mortar as possible, since cousin Bert owns the kiln and nephew Phineas has the cement works. In programming, someone has to find a way to use up all those megabytes of RAM and gigabytes of hard disk. We would hate to see the power of the Pentium go unused.

End users may actually be hindered by too much real computational power anyway. They are blinded by blinding speed. What they really want is to see things happening; they want scintillating screens, prancing pictographs, and flickering flames. The appearance of action is more important than accomplishment, and, by golly, the Contrarion Conspiracy stands ready to see that Parkinson's Law is honored by seeking sophisticated solutions, which means unnecessarily complex ones. Project groups are deliberately organized to work at cross purposes, because this guarantees redundant features and internal incompatibilities, ensuring a high degree of needless complexity.

Dear reader, do not doubt me. Do not dismiss this as the paranoid palaver of a mad methodologist! The proof of this diabolism is right in front of you. On the very windows of your wondrous machines are splattered the cabalistic symbols of their programmatic perversion, in the chevrons of maximization and minimization, in the bars of control, in the windmills of waiting states.

Devil You Say

Proof you ask for, proof you get. My office mate and I have been checking out Windows-based Personal Information Managers. One in particular is so fiendishly clever, with its cutesy DayTimer™ simulation and profligate use of screen real estate, that only a Contrarion Conspiracy could have produced it.

Deletion is the definitively damning datum: you delete an item from your notebook by dragging it to a wire wastebasket icon. (Yes, *wire!*) Then the wastebasket bursts into flames! Iconic immolation! Major programming resources were wasted on this software basket case. But it is so *cute!* It really impresses upper management, purchasing agents, and other mental defectives. Few, however, have discovered that, on a fast 486 with an accelerated video board and a large-screen monitor, the fast flickering flames are seen to form the perfect likeness of the late Lawrence Welk! Need I say more?

The software development methods of the conspiracy reflect and serve its goals. The best practitioners announce a product, then design the box, then begin coding. Flow charting is tough. Flow charts are much easier to draw from existing code, so contrarion project teams start by coding low-level routines, such as display drivers and flaming icons, around which they organize everything else and from which they derive flow charts for the overall processing. Once the software is in beta test, the system requirements can be written as the foreword to the manual.

Beware, because a Contrarion Conspiracy may masquerade as an ordinary R&D group or project team, but in clandestine meetings held after 10 P.M. they plan their deviant development scenarios. Have you ever wondered about some of your programming buddies who work so late? Odds are they have been inducted into the secret rites of the Contrarion Conspiracy, which celebrates its 666th anniversary on the first of April 1993.

---

* From the e-mail responses I got, not all readers took into account the April Fools dateline of this piece when it was originally published.

IV

Tools and Methods

Introduction

Our distant ancestors were dubbed *homo habilis*, "man, the tool maker." Human beings are not nature's only tool makers, but it is certainly an essential expression of our relation to the world around us. We extend our reach through tools. We see the unseeable, move the unmovable, manipulate the microscopic, and construct the gargantuan. We write programs, which are at once invisible and enormous. Many common trades and activities would be all but impossible in their modern form were it not for good tools. Carpentry, mechanics, civil engineering, aeronautics, electronics, cooking — all have their kits of essential tools and their methods of application.

The tools of any trade evolve over time with changes in practice and materials. There was a time when you could recognize an engineer coming toward you by the ubiquitous slide rule hanging in its belt case. When I started programming, the standard tools were a coding sheet, a plastic flow-charting template, and a core dump. We wrote in FORTRAN or assembler and never laid hands on the computer itself. A big program was a tray of cards: 4,000 lines of code. If you were good, you could hold it in your head. Elaborate tools for modeling, design, and debugging were neither available nor needed.

But things changed. The typical programmer now can have an array of favorite tools for every phase of development, from conception through debugging and installation. In this section we'll explore some aspects of the relationship between programmers and their tools.

CASE and Cognition[*]

Computer-Aided Software Engineering, CASE, is no longer the hottest topic in software and applications development. Even the vendors of CASE tools are retitling their products, calling them "integrated development environments" or just "tool suites." Whatever they are called, the development tools we use or fail to use can have a lot to do with what we accomplish as developers.

I happen to be a strong proponent of tools. Admittedly, many of those available today are relatively primitive, often misconceived systems produced by misguided tool vendors who neither understand nor use the software engineering methodologies their tools support. Still, they can be effective tools in much the same way that a stone ax beats bare hands for felling trees.

Not surprisingly, you often hear something like this: "We don't have time to use CASE; we have a deadline to meet." Some of these protesters are the same programmers, now balding or graying, who resisted higher level languages. They probably never flow chart or draw a data flow diagram and will insist that they, unlike us ordinary mortals, can keep track of everything in

[*] From *Computer Language Magazine*, Volume 9, #1, January 1992.

their heads. On the other hand, many critics of CASE tools really do try to practice some kind of reasonable design and development discipline. Unfortunately, many of the CASE tools, rather than helping the process of methodical problem solving or creative engineering, actually hinder it.

What's wrong with this picture? You see a high-salary software engineer, in an office with a six-thousand-dollar workstation, running a twelve-thousand-dollar CASE tool, and he's drawing on his desk pad, making notes on a yellow tablet of recycled notepaper. Finally, after much crossing out, erasing, and redrawing, he puts mitt to mouse and begins to enter what he's worked out, effectively reducing the sophisticated tool suite on his workstation to an elaborate electronic drafting board.

What's wrong is this: Rather than working with the software engineer and how engineers think, the tool is probably working against him. Instead of supporting natural ability and the habits sharpened through training, the CASE tool is interfering with them. To understand the exact nature of this failure, we need to look at how people, especially engineer-type people, solve problems.

Sketching

We know, for example, that many of the better software engineers, analysts, and designers do their finest work by sketching out a broad-brushed picture of what they want to do, then going back to fill in details or elaborate. Look over the shoulder of such a problem solver and watch what she does. She might start a design by drawing a whole collection of component symbols. Then she begins to fill in the relationships among some of these blank boxes, drawing lines and arrows among them. Finally, she labels the components and specifies some details of the interconnections.

What about typical CASE tools? In many of them, you select a diagram symbol with the mouse from a collection of icons, position the cursor, again with the mouse, where you want the symbol to appear in the diagram being developed, and then click to drop the symbol in place. At this point, a dialogue box opens up and asks you to name the thing, which you must do in compliance with whatever general and corporate standards are being enforced for the naming of such symbols. Next you are called on to describe it, specify its interfaces, and maybe choose among several variants. Only after all this is completed in conformance with the syntax checking in force are you allowed to return to the drawing. By this time you have probably forgotten what you earlier knew you were going to do next. Worse, the general conception of the content and structure of the problem that seemed so clear when you reached for the mouse is now lost, erased from your mental map by the CASE tool's preoccupation with distracting details.

Alternatives and Alternative Views

All engineering is trade-offs. There is research going back over thirty years showing that more effective engineers typically compare two or more alternative approaches to each significant design problem. This strategy applies just as well to software engineering as to our older sister professions. (My thesis at M.I.T. was on just this subject.) The comparison between alternative approaches may be quick and mostly mental, or it may involve elaborate description and modeling of each alternative, with careful analysis and evaluation of the consequences. A clear winning strategy may emerge, but sometimes what is chosen is a creative synthesis of more than one alternative, sometimes a compromise. The essential part of the process is the weighing of alternatives, being able to eyeball two designs or interpretations side-by-side. Current CASE tools do not, for the most part, support having two versions of the same system, diagram, or model simultaneously active and accessible, certainly not for side-by-side comparisons.

I've seen some pretty clever subterfuges used to get around this limitation of CASE tools. At one firm, a systems analyst had two workstations in his office, one processing a dummy project record, so that he could keep two full-fledged versions of the same systems design in front of him to analyze their advantages and disadvantages. More commonly, one of the alternatives is on paper, the other in the CASE repository.

Here's a scenario you may have seen or acted out yourself. The software engineer using a CASE tool tells the tool to print or plot one model of the system being designed, perhaps a data flow diagram, runs down the hall to the print server and retrieves the output, then returns to the office to call up another model of the same system, maybe a structure chart. The software engineer then keeps going back and forth between the model on the screen and the one on the paper.

Even the so-called "integrated" CASE "tool suites" do not generally support simple, rapid shifting among alternative views or models of the same system-in-progress. It should be at most a keystroke between views. Better yet would be true, side-by-side comparison. And windows just don't quite cut it. By the time you have two windows up in a CASE tool that operates in a windowed mode or environment, there isn't enough screen left to actually see anything useful. Either you get a little peek at a small part of each diagram, or you get an overview of tiny, unreadable symbols and text. Hardly a computer aid to software engineering!

Creation and Evaluation

Among the worst offenders in interfering with the thought processes of software developers are some of the more advanced tools, such as the context-sensitive program editors that do syntax checking on entry, or the CASE tools that support and enforce a software development "methodology" by constraining the CASE user to entering only proper diagrams and descriptions in precisely the order defined by some definitive text by some definitive methodology guru.

In the early days of computer-supported word processing, spell-checkers were separate programs, so slow and inefficient that you never checked a document more than absolutely necessary, and often you "forgot." But, the computers and the search techniques got faster. Spell-checkers were integrated with the word processors. Pretty soon some programmer with time on his hands thought of doing spell-checking "on-the-fly," as words were actually being entered. After all, during text entry, the processor is idle most of the time anyway, and the lookup can proceed, letter by letter, between keystrokes. Clever idea, right? Wrong!

If you have ever used a word processor or electronic typewriter with a real-time spell-checker, you know. The little gremlin is constantly interrupting to tell you about some alleged misspelling, popping up like an over-eager puppy or beeping liking a bar-code scanner at the grocery checkout. Even when it is right and you're wrong, you don't care, you just want to get your thoughts on paper without being interrupted by the mishuganah spell-checking smarty.

One of the rules of the simple but powerful technique of brainstorming is that no one is allowed to criticize or comment on any idea until the entire process is completed and all ideas are on the table. Separating the process of creation from the process of evaluation improves problem solving.

A CASE tool that fits with how people think would not criticize while you are creating. In fact, it would allow you to draw and specify all sorts of things that "aren't proper" because these "framebreaking" departures from the rules are often crucial steps along the way to finding better solutions. And it would allow you to depart from the prescribed sequence for entering things, because the "methodologies" in the books are not necessarily the last word on software engineering. (In fact, many methodologies are really quite wrong in terms of human problem solving, but that's another subject.)

Should we abandon hope and leave the CASE tools on the shelf? No, there's still hope. Present-day CASE tools are the primitive precursors of the tools we really need. They'll evolve.

It's a little like the early word processing programs, such as Electric Pencil or the first versions of WordStar. By today's standards of functionality and convenience, they were not much. You had to wait for minutes to go between one end of a document and another, the keystrokes to accomplish common tasks were obscure and complicated, and format control was limited, but they were so very much better than handwriting on foolscap or typing and retyping and retyping.

Besides, some of those who create CASE tools may be listening.

19

Modeling Matters*

"A good development tool is one that doesn't slow me down." The programmer looked warily at the eighty-pound box holding the latest and greatest in C++ development environments. "What I really want is one that lets me just get on with programming the way I want to, then it takes the code and generates those stupid diagrams that my boss insists on having." As I watch, I'm thinking that maybe it's time we talked about those stupid diagrams.

Many developers, especially those who cut their coding teeth on microcomputers and workstations, take a pretty dim view of structure charts, object communication diagrams, data flow diagrams, and flow charts. Quite a few of them have never drawn a functional hierarchy and wouldn't know what to do with one if it was lying on the desk. To them, a Booch-gram is bad news delivered on yellow paper by a courier from Booch Telecommunications.

To many of today's software wizards, those boxes and bubbles and clouds and arrows look like the hieroglyphics of a vanished priesthood, the legacy of moribund methods, like structured analysis and design, that have been superseded by streamlined object-oriented rapid prototyping. Charts and diagrams have no place in the fast-paced world of hack-and-backslash micro applications and software development using visual programming and rapid application development. "We don't have time to draw pictures; we have a release date to meet!" "Why would anyone ever draw diagrams when they

* From *Software Development,* Volume 2, #2, February 1994.

could be cutting code?" It's a good question. Why does anyone do those drawings?

Of course, structure charts and other classic design and analysis models were not developed to slow down programming, any more than they were created to satisfy fussy customers or to keep meddling managers happy. Most were developed by developers for their own use in order to simplify and speed up their work. Time spent thinking about programs through models is time saved programming and debugging. By allowing the software developer to model programs without having to code them, by making it easier to lay out the organization of intricate solutions for complex problems, analysis and design models shorten development time. All this is well established and well known. Good design cuts development time; good design models simplify design.

Not all graphical models work this way in practice. Some, like IBM's HIPO charts and its companion methods, have died a well-deserved death. Others were impeded by the clumsiness or complexity of the notation or the mechanics of drawing them. CASE tools first arrived on the scene primarily as specialized drawing tools to make the drafting of diagrams easier. Over time they evolved into more comprehensive aids to software engineering.

Picture This

Software developers draw pictures when they could be writing real programs for much the same reasons that architects draw floor plans and elevations before building a house. Buildings were not always built from plans and drawings, though. If a building is simple enough and familiar enough, crews can work without models, figuring out the design as they go along. The turn-of-the-century rural community didn't need blueprints to raise a barn. Those old barns were simple designs and used simplified construction methods. Everyone knew what a barn looked like, how it was constructed, and what was needed to build it. Most of the community had done it before, and any first-timers could learn just by paying attention and doing what they saw others do. But when you go from yerts and barns to four-bedroom garrison colonials or high-rise apartment complexes, things get more complex.

And so it is with computer programs. Back when 64K of RAM was the limit and CP/M was the operating environment, keeping an entire program in your head may have been possible and sensible. But anyone who says they can keep track of and make sense of the details in a hundred thousand lines of

C code is lying — if not to you, then to themselves. This is where design models come in.

Note that we are talking about models, not diagrams, about design, not documentation. To many software developers, those odd little pictures are ends in themselves, at best only another form of documentation, something to be stored in a binder because the contract requires it. Design models can indeed be useful as documentation. The blueprints for your house not only guided the contractors but can help show where to cut into a wall to find — or avoid — a hot water pipe. Structure charts and block communication diagrams can tell you where to look for particular procedures or to trace the flow of information or to understand how a completed system was laid out. But the main purpose of design models is to help in design.

Managing Complexity

A model, at least any reasonable model, is simpler than the thing it models. Using a good modeling notation, the important features and characteristics of a very complex system can be represented in a relatively small and simple diagram.

Modeling gives mental leverage. If you know the symbols and the language, the model can be a way of picturing and then thinking about complex problems, especially in terms of the relationships among pieces. In code or text, relationships are implicit; a word or label here refers to a thing that is elsewhere. In most graphical models, relationships are explicit, visible as those lines and arrows connecting parts of the diagram. Good graphical models can also offer a meaningful overview of a system that would be impossible to get from reading — or writing — page after page of code.

Of course, many people create purely mental models of problems they are working on. Some experienced developers may even visualize systems through structural diagrams they keep in their heads. Diagrams on paper or on a screen still have advantages because they externalize the internal mental models. External models become stable and can be reflected upon or compared to other models. An externalized model can be set aside and re-examined later from a fresh perspective. Often times, seeing something committed to lines and boxes changes how you think about it, suggesting other possibilities or causing mistakes or oversights to become more obvious. And no one else can see the model you have in your head, but an entire project team can study and work on the model on the wall or in the CASE tool repository.

Good modeling tools also allow for a kind of sketching that is difficult in code. Programming languages are precise and detailed and compilers stubbornly insist on exact syntax and completed constructs. A whiteboard has no such constraints. A developer or group can gather around and play with the pictures, moving things around and tracing out complex paths over widely separated regions of the system. In short, design models allow software engineers to act more like real engineers, trying out and comparing alternative ways to organize software without having to reduce ideas to code.

Almost any aspect of software can be modeled graphically: algorithm, data structure, communication, composition, dynamics. For each of these and others there may be dozens of competing notations and conventions. But one model is not necessarily as good as another. Notations vary tremendously in their ability to carry meaning. It matters what shape the blobs are and which way the arrows point.

How do you tell the good from the bad from the ugly? Stay tuned.

20

Mirror, Mirror[*]

Mirror, mirror, on the wall, who's the fairest of them all? The wicked queen in *Snow White* had only to look in her mirror to get the true picture. Software engineers should be so lucky. They need good mirrors that simply and accurately reflect the software being engineered. The wicked queen may have been displeased by what she learned, but at least her mirror gave a true image with no difficulty in interpretation.

That's what a good modeling notation offers: a clear image of software — unambiguous and easy to interpret. Unlike a looking glass, a useful modeling notation cannot simply reflect a detailed picture with a one-to-one correspondence to code. A good model is an accurate but selective embodiment of software, a necessarily simplified picture. The effectiveness of a modeling notation for expressing problems and their software solutions depends on how this simplification is achieved. The precise nature of the translation between the medium of the programming language and the medium of the modeling notation should be simple, straightforward, logical, and easy to learn.

Unfortunately, many of today's proliferating program analysis and design notations fail in these fundamental requirements. They are overly complex, arbitrary, ambiguous, difficult to learn, and difficult to interpret. And, of course, there are far too many of them.

Complete modeling of software is complicated, involving numerous views of static and dynamic aspects: the structure and composition of information, the

[*] From *Software Development,* Volume 2, #3, March 1994.

nature of the algorithms and their realization as procedures, factoring into component parts, and communication among parts. If the data model, procedural model, communication model, state model, and functional composition of software are all conflated into a single diagram in one comprehensive notation, the result is baroque, visually cluttered, and hard to understand.

Getting the Picture

Software engineering models serve much the same purposes as the wicked queen's mirror. Notations should make clear the difference between the fairest of solutions and those that are only fair. Developers need to be able to tell by looking at a model whether the design is sound or stupid. A software design model is not merely a holding place for as-yet-unbuilt software ideas. It allows developers to spot problems and shortcomings in the design and to compare approaches to see which is superior. Ultimately this is why good developers draw pictures before they code — it's cheaper to build paper models than to build software, and good models make it easier to see how to do things well.

Good notation allows for simple, direct, and unambiguous translation between model and code: to develop code from a model and to model existing code. Sloppy, obscure, or imprecise notation makes for sloppy, obscure, and imprecise translation. Every visual element in the notation should correspond with some specific and relevant aspect of the software being modeled; every important feature in the code should be expressible in the notation.

A good notation produces pictures that can be interpreted analytically, through a thorough study of details, and understood intuitively as a gestalt — a whole representing the overall character of a system. Complicated designs should look more complicated than simple ones, good architecture should be more visually appealing than bad design. In other words, a good notation allows developers to use both sides of the brain; it helps them think both logically and intuitively about the system being designed.

To accurately mirror software, yet present a substantially simplified view, good notation highlights things that are important and hides or suppresses those that are not. Dominant features and major components are writ large, while minor details are annotations or disappear from view.

The picture is kept simple by not showing internal details. A software component that is basically a black box becomes a simple box drawn on screen or paper; internal details are invisible. Lines pointing to these graphical boxes suggest programming references to software boxes, not to their internal features.

Ideally, we want the kind of selective control over visibility only possible in a computerized tool. We would like, for instance, to browse through an object communication diagram, skimming over a landscape of tiny objects, then zoom in to study relationships in one region. We might close in on one object to see what methods it supports. We double-click and are looking at the C++ code defining one method. Or we might flip to a view that superimposes user interaction scenarios on the communication diagram, highlighting or coloring objects participating in one scenario.

Notation and Usability

It's easy to develop your own notation; all too many people do. It's hard to do it well, and many notations that fill our journals and magazines are not very good as modeling tools.

Designing a good notation is like designing a good user interface. The goal is to reduce human memory load. The Great Law of Usability says a system should be usable — without training, assistance, or manuals — by someone who knows the application but not the software (Constantine 1991b). A really good notation, then, is one that an experienced software engineer who knows how to design and build software can interpret directly and intuitively without a week-long class or a complicated cheat-sheet. You shouldn't have to remember arbitrary things like a double-barred box as a dynamic object or one with a flag in the corner as a reused library component.

Things should look like what they are. Symbol shapes and line styles cannot be arbitrary or counter-intuitive. For instance, the basic foundation upon which other components are built through inheritance and reuse should look like solid and well-defined elements, not ephemeral clouds.

Strong connections between parts should look strong; weaker ones should look more tenuous. Stable objects should appear solid, dynamic ones should convey some sense of activity or changeability. For example, inheritance by one class of the features and characteristics of another means that the subclass is strongly dependent on the superclass, just as a child's genetic characteristics are strongly dependent on those of both parents. To accurately reflect the characteristics of software using it, inheritance should be shown in a way that looks stronger than message passing or reference to an object as an attribute (Page-Jones, Constantine, and Weiss 1990).

What makes a notation intuitive and easy to learn can be a matter of small and subtle details. In Jacobson's notation for object-oriented software (Jacobson et al. 1992), objects that interface with the outside have a "lazy-tee" (⊢) on one side as a visual reminder of the interface. Dynamic objects that control sequences of interaction have an arrowhead imbedded in the border, suggesting a loop or iteration. In several notations, internal features of components that are externally accessible are shown straddling the border of the component.

A good notation also builds on and uses what software engineers already know, especially what they know about notations. That means not using new symbols for old concepts and not recycling the same pictures for new and incompatible ideas. In fact, we probably don't need any new notations. Our efforts would be better spent standardizing and consolidating what we already have, applying sound principles of modeling and human thought.

Think about it.

21

Methodical Madness[*]

As if all those dumb diagrams were not enough to bury the busy programmer, every model seems to come with its own method attached. Structured methods may no longer be cool beans, but there seems to be no shortage of newcomers to fill bookshelves and journals and conference programs. These latest and greatest methods may be rapid and reuse objects for prototypes, but there is much that is vaguely familiar about even the most radical of the new development methods.

There's no real mystery to software methods. You, too, can be a software methodologist, without even taking a correspondence course. Whether it's called structured analysis and design, information engineering, or round-trip gestalt, whether it's object-oriented or just plain vanilla procedural programming, behind all the books and the babble, it all boils down to systematic problem solving. By furnishing a framework for orderly use of models and tools, methods can make the software development process more repeatable, which means easier to learn and easier to refine and improve.

Underlying all major software analysis and design methods is a very small set of basic principles, repeatedly rediscovered and recast in ever fresh vocabulary, but still just the same old shinola. It's all based on how human beings solve complex problems. The five principles underlying all software engineering methods are: (1) orderly progression, (2) solution by subdivision, (3) component independence, (4) component integrity, and (5) structural fit.

[*] From *Software Development*, Volume 2, #5, May 1994.

Step One

The important thing in getting a big job done is to start someplace, do something, then do something else. Methods give you a place to start and someplace to go next. Each step in the process takes you, with hope in your heart and code in your head, one step closer to a finished software solution.

All methods give you some kind of orderly recipe that outlines all the things you will have to do to complete the work and deliver the software. They serve as a reminder of the various matters that must be considered and understood in order to develop systems. Good methods put first things first and defer the deferrable. This is the principle of orderly progression at work: do this, then that, then this.

Subdivide

All *real* software problems, the sort that programming professionals confront daily in their jobs, are too big and complicated to solve. The only completely solvable programming problems are those toy applications and academic exercises found in textbooks and taught in all-day tutorials. This is one reason why academic computer scientists can waste entire careers on elegant mathematics and methods of formal proof that are hopelessly inadequate to everyday programming problems. They never see real problems.

We do. When confronted by unmanageable complexity, what do we do? The same thing our primitive ancestors did when faced with a haunch of mastodon too big to swallow: we bite off a chunk and start chewing. We tackle big problems by breaking them up into little ones. It's a bit of mental magic, hand waving that does not really make the true enormity of software problems go away. But it often works anyway, giving the overloaded developer the illusion that big, complex systems can be built out of lots of small, simple pieces of code.

Sometimes, like the hapless little apprentice sorcerer, we find that chopping up one big problem only compounds our problems. Big problems become smaller when chopped up only to the extent that the little pieces don't have much to do with each other and can be approached more or less independently, each designed and programmed as a manageable little software exercise in itself. All effective software engineering methods include some form of rules or guidance that tells you to make clean cuts when you carve up the problem, separating the total into independent bits, each of which makes sense as a distinct subproblem.

There are really two problem-solving principles rolled up into one here. The principle of component independence says you should subdivide the problem into loosely related subproblems. The principle of component integrity says each of the pieces should make sense as an integral whole.

In traditional structured design, these principles are embodied in the venerable concepts of coupling and cohesion. Coupling is a measure of the degree of interaction and interdependence between software components; cohesion is a measure of the degree to which a component comprises a well-defined functional whole. These old concepts have been rediscovered in the fresh world of object technology. Good object-oriented methods remind programmers to reduce object coupling and to raise the cohesion of methods by encapsulating all the right goodies in each object basket. Otherwise you end up with a tortuous tangle of interwoven objects that defy analysis and resist reuse.

Structural Fit

These first principles of complex problem solving are all concerned with individual pieces of software, but do not say much about how these parts are best organized into a working whole. Most methods tell us in one form or another to look to the real world, to emulate the structure of the problem in the structure of our solution. In other words, the software should be organized along the same lines as the "real-world" problem it is supposed to solve. This is the principle of structural fit, software engineering's version of the bauhaus dictum that form should follow from function.

This principle gets its most radical realization in the more simplistic methods of object technology that say all you have to do is look at the real world and construct object classes for whatever you see "out there." Here's a chair, there's a chair — tada, we create class chair, with superclass furniture. Following this advice too blindly leads to clumsy translations of physical systems into klutzy software. And then there's the problem that your reality and mine may have little overlap.

Still, the basic premise is sound. Reflecting the "natural" structure of the problem domain in software saves us from solving problems that don't need solving. Instead of inventing whole new architectures, we use the serviceable ones that already exist "out there." By sticking to the structure of the problem domain, maintenance, expansion, and reuse are all made easier because the software is simply structured the way people already think about the problem.

That's it. Methods are the frameworks for using models to solve software problems.

Of course, it takes a lot more to have a real method and justify calling yourself a real methodologist. You have to be good at making up words. You need a lot of new vocabulary or people will think they already know what you are trying to teach. And you have to be able to stretch a few good ideas into 700 pages of textbook. And don't forget the notation, those clever little shapes that make your method recognizable among its many competitors. But be careful not to make the pictures too simple or the principles too transparent, or you won't be able to justify those training and consulting fees!

V

Process Improvements

Introduction

Producing software is a process. Applications do not just happen, programs do not simply spring full-blown from the brains of programmers. This is a good thing, since one of the basic principles of the modern "quality" movement is that processes can be improved. Indeed, the goal in the so-called "total quality" movement and its various incarnations in the software world is not just improvements in steps or fits or bursts, but continuous process improvement. The most advanced organizations not only study the processes by which software and applications are produced, but have instituted programs for feeding their findings back into the process in a closed loop that refines their systems and procedures continuously.

Achieving this somewhat utopian ideal of nonstop improvement can take a major corporate commitment. Companies that embark on this journey toward software engineering enlightenment often start with an expensive and elaborate appraisal of their current culture and practices. They may hire consultants to evaluate their organization using something like the Capability Maturity Model developed by the Software Engineering Institute, an elaborate rating that boils down to a number from 1 to 5. If all you want to do is find out how mature your organization is, you can save your money. Probably you are at Level 1, meaning your processes are lousy and unreliable but you don't even know quite how lousy or unreliable because you don't measure anything. Almost everyone is at Level 1, so this is a fairly safe bet. (If you want, I'll come visit and send you a bill before announcing the foregone conclusion.)

The real reason for going through the pain and expense of a more elaborate and formal assessment is not to find out a number but to learn in some detail where and how things are going wrong and where you can start creating institutionalized practices that will make things better. Maybe after some years of effort — and more money to consultants — you will reach Level 3. Rumors of a rare Level 5 software engineering group being spotted in the wilds of rural Virginia are frequently referenced but remain unconfirmed. Do not misinterpret my casual stance. I am not knocking consultants — I am one myself, after all — nor am I questioning the potential payoffs of thorough organizational assessments; in fact, my firm does such assessments for clients. And I am most emphatically *not* opposed to software developers being prepared to invest substantial sums and resources in process improvement. But I do want to make clear that I think there may be other ways to create improved processes, ways that are not as dramatic, do not cost as much, and are not quite so high profile.

This section will look at some of these simple ideas and modest proposals for improving software quality through better development processes. There are no major social programs here, nothing that could justify astronomical consulting fees for business process re-engineering, just things that small groups and even individual developers and managers can do to do a better job.

The Benefits of Visibility*

I remember writing my first program, a FORTRAN exercise for a course known as 6.41. Everything went by the numbers at M.I.T. in those days, and so did my program. It was a breeze to write, it just didn't compile the first time. Or the second. I was devastated and dumbfounded. When I finally did get it to compile, I was utterly shocked to find out it didn't work. I couldn't see why; it looked right to me. I showed it to my roommate. Marshall was a math major. I think he was writing algorithms before there were computers to run them on.

"I can't figure out what's wrong with this program, see, it's supposed to…" He grabbed the print-out, what we affectionately called an 80-80 listing, for reasons that only those who remember punched cards will know.

"What's that?" He jabbed with his stubby Brooklyn finger.

"Looks like a C."

"You don't want it there." He was right. The statement still compiled, but the computer wasn't reading it the way I had intended. Marshall went back to something having to do with gradients and del operators, all the while polishing

---

* From *Computer Language Magazine*, Volume 9, #2, 1992.

his interpretation of Marlon Brando in *A Streetcar Named Desire.* What I learned from this was never to show Marshall anything I ever wrote, especially code. He would always find something wrong with it, and I had yet to reach the point where I could regard this as a favor. Besides, it invariably seemed to inspire another bout of his bellowing out, "Stella, Stella!" There was a lesson lurking here, but I wasn't ready for it. Eventually, of course, I caught on to the fact that running a problem past a fellow programmer was often the most efficient way to find some elusive bug or to work out some tricky algorithm. In fact, most of us learn that talking out our ideas, using a colleague as a sounding board or getting feedback on something still half-jelled, is not only effective and enriches the end product, but it's also fun and builds good working relationships.

Dynamic Duos

It took P. J. Plauger, though, to really teach me about the benefits of visibility. Shortly after he started Whitesmiths, Ltd., I visited him at their New York "headquarters," a small apartment in Manhattan. Somewhere off in one of the rooms there lurked a minicomputer, stuffed in a closet in order to keep the clatter down was a printer, and around what should have been the living room were scattered several terminals. At each terminal were two programmers!

Of course, only one programmer was actually cutting code at each keyboard, but the others were peering over their shoulders, doing those annoying things that New Yorkers are especially schooled in, namely kibitzing. The room buzzed with a steady stream of questions about the algorithm or whether an initial value was correct, suggestions about how to break out of a loop, or drawing attention to a syntax error or a test done in the wrong order or a missing case. After awhile the two programmers would switch places, and the one at the keyboard would become the professional nudge.

I speculated about cash flow problems being at the root of their shortage of hardware, but Plauger assured me that this was their chosen mode for working. Pretty inefficient, huh? Nope. Having adopted this approach, they were delivering finished and tested code faster than ever. A closer look showed why. The code that came out the back of these two-programmer terminals was nearly 100% bug-free. Not only did it have fewer defects, but it was better code, tighter and more efficient, having benefited from the thinking of two bright minds and the steady dialogue between trusted terminal-mates. I came to think of this model for programming teamwork as the "Dynamic Duo." The principle operating here is very broad: Increasing work visibility leads to increased quality! Two programmers in tandem is not redundancy; it's a direct route to greater efficiency and better quality.

The same principle applies to learning. Most people — not all, but most — learn more rapidly in small groups than they do alone. This is even true of many diehards who are convinced that they can't learn that way or who hate to work in groups. There are numerous contributing factors. Discussion brings up issues and ideas that might never have occurred to the isolated individual. Peers can often explain and interpret difficult concepts when an instructor cannot. New ideas and approaches emerge from the dialogue itself. Perhaps most basically, students in groups learn from each other, not just from an instructor or textbook. It's one of the reasons I nearly always use project and study teams in the workshops and seminars that I lead.

The rule seems to apply particularly to learning a programming language. Plauger has observed that, for language learning, there seems to be an optimum number of students per terminal. It's not one. It's probably two. Three also works, but one student working alone generally learns the language significantly more slowly than when paired up with a partner. At the other end of the scale, four or more working at one computer are always getting in each other's way — figuratively and physically. Groups this large often end up splitting into subgroups or will resort to "time sharing" and ultimately prove less effective. So if you really want to add C++ or Smalltalk to your repertoire, don't closet yourself with the manual and a tutorial program. Grab a programming buddy and sit down together at one keyboard. Knowing this principle may also offer new hope for budget-bound schools and for companies whose training departments have just been laid off.

Virtual Visibility

Interestingly, to get the benefit of work visibility, it may not always be necessary for anyone else even to say a word. Most of us have had some experience with one of those perversely elusive bugs. You study the test run and the listing, and you know that the problem is somewhere in one particular block of code, but no matter how many times you walk through that section, you can't find where it blows up. So you bang on the door of the next office and hang-doggedly ask for some help. Charlotte, after all, has a Ph.D. in Computer Science. You start to describe the background of the problem. As you explain the loop to her, something leaps out at you. Before she can say anything, you sigh a quiet "Oh!" then back sheepishly out the door as you mutter thanks. "Any time," she replies.

The very act of explaining or describing something to someone else seems to alter our thought patterns. I don't know if it is actually necessary to have someone else in the room. Perhaps it is sufficient to imagine you are explaining the problem to someone else, but I suspect it's never quite as good solo.

Like all guidelines to building better systems, the Principle of Work Visibility can be carried too far. One form of this particular reduction to an absurdity (or should it be expansion to an absurdity?) is the programming model that seems to be favored by certain major software vendors, what might be called the "mongrel horde" approach to program development. The formula is simple. Just get a lot of programmers and put them in a big room, a programming bull pit with acres of desks and terminals and everything in on-line databases and e-mail threads for all to read and remark upon. We all know what comes out of this approach.

The benefits of visibility in most situations leap by large quanta when a second person is put into the process, but the returns diminish with successive additions. There are exceptions, of course, for special kinds of activities, especially in the very early or late stages of system development. Brainstorming generally works better with more brains to whip up the storm; small groups may only manage to churn up a dust devil or two or may even sit around becalmed. Code or design walkthroughs also seem to benefit from the contributions of many reviewers walking through, the many eyes being all the better to spot the problems or weaknesses. On the other hand, for real problem solving, wrestling with intricately interwoven sets of constraints, and puzzling out a good software architecture, too many heads often end up butting up against each other. Generally speaking, this is probably yet another of those seven-plus-or-minus-twoish things, where maximum scale is modest.

Structured Views

The principle of work visibility reaches its zenith in some of the specialized teamwork and group models designed for software development. In Joint Application Design, or JAD (Wood and Silver 1989), a group of end users and developers work out requirements analysis and high-level design through a highly structured meeting process. The visibility of the process to the users and their chance to furnish input in an active way lead to better systems and improved rapport between communities of system users and system developers.

The so-called structured open team described in Chapter 21 (Constantine 1989; Thomsett 1990) is another model that exploits the principle of visibility to improve system quality and, ultimately, development efficiency. In such a development team, project members do a large portion of their work in each other's presence throughout the life cycle. Marc Rettig (1990) reports that one successful team spent half of each work day meeting as a group. Of course, these were not merely meetings as we usually think of them, but working sessions. The purpose was not to review minutes or keep each other apprised of progress, but actually to do work. In structured open teamwork, people analyze problems, design modules, and even work out coding details in groups. These working sessions are facilitated by a team member to make them more efficient and effective, but much of the real power comes from the visibility that the open process brings to software development.

Any software development group can improve software quality just by finding ways to increase visibility in the programming process. There will be detractors and resistors, of course. We all know programmers who come and go at odd hours when nobody is around, who encrypt their source files, and who hunch over their terminals to keep anyone who happens to walk by from peeking at their programs.

But remember, the Stealth Programmer is a disappearing breed.

23

Rewards and Reuse [*]

We recycle so many things, from grocery bags to toner cartridges, why not recycle code? Why not reuse our designs and models rather than always starting from scratch? The rewards of reuse seem to be enormous. What code is cheaper to write than the code you don't have to write at all? With higher levels of reuse supported by larger component libraries, we might double or triple effective productivity. All we have to do is change the whole culture of software development and maybe the personalities of programmers.

Old Problems

Reuse is hardly a new idea. The lowly subroutine was conceived so that the same instructions did not have to be written out each time a particular calculation was needed. Reusable component libraries have been around for almost as long as people have been programming. The first to yield to reuse were math routines, followed soon by input-output. Except for the sheer joy or perversity of doing it, no applications or tool developer writes their own sine-cosine routines anymore.

Then, what is the problem? Unfortunately, most programmers like to program. Some of them would rather program than eat or bathe. Most of them would much rather cut code than chase documentation or search catalogs or try to figure out some other stupid programmer's idiotic work. Software developers

[*] From *Computer Language Magazine*, Volume 9, #7, 1992.

develop things; users use them. Other things being equal, programmers will design and build from scratch rather than recycle. All of them are convinced that they can write it tighter or faster or more elegantly than whoever came before. So, even though it might make them more productive, programmers are almost constitutionally biased against reuse. How do we encourage them to change their habits? Suddenly the chorus in the balcony starts singing contrapuntally: "Incentives. Market forces. Rewards schemes. Royalties. Reinforcement schedules. Culture change." Such lovely cacophony.

Lending Support

It really is not all that hard to understand the score. Reuse on any substantial scale begins with reusable component libraries. There are really only two basic problems involved in such libraries: getting things into them and getting things out again! For programmers to reuse components from a library, there must first be components in the library. Where do these come from?

Various models have been proposed and tried. One is simply to accept free donations from anyone willing to have their code published in the library. Some organizations have had trouble getting donations until they either offered to pay for them or at least promised that authors would not be hounded for maintenance or modification. This approach, a sort of "used-book store" model, appears to be inexpensive, building a large library with little or no direct investment in component development. In theory, components are generated as a side effect of regular development projects.

It does work, but the libraries typically resemble the familiar used-book store. I have spent many happy hours pawing through stacks and boxes of used books, but I think of this more as recreation than as a model for information retrieval or code recycling.

Typically there is little or no quality control and no accountability with this approach. To induce donations, contributing programmers are absolved of responsibility. What you need may be in there, but the odds are against finding it. If it takes the typical programmer more than 2 minutes and 27 seconds to find something, they will conclude it does not exist and therefore will reinvent it.

Components in libraries built with this open enrollment approach are like those thousands of old books of varied vintages and values heaped in disarray. Browsing through the dusty piles for an unexpected treasure can be great fun, but you would not want to do so on a tight deadline. If you know that you need a good current source on post-Soviet economics, you would go to a well-stocked and organized university bookstore, not the basement book-seller with the diverse exotica.

Meilir Page-Jones tells of a client whose "used-book" component library grew so unwieldy that they decided to appoint a reuse librarian whose job it was to keep things *out* of the component library, letting only the finest become part of the repository. Legend has it that this person became known as Conan the Librarian. For this approach to work, however, there must be sub-stantial forces impelling developers to donate to the library.

Programming Royalty

Some companies, on the other hand, are biting the bullet of up-front costs and forming groups of full-time developers whose function it is to build compo-nents for reuse. These are not typical grunt coders, but highly skilled specialists with a knack for recognizing commonalities, defining abstractions, and build-ing bullet-proof code covering just the right domain. They are rewarded for creating quality components with high potential for reuse. They may even get royalties for each use made of one of their contributions to the library.

If such developers are simply salaried, it could be in their interest to build fancier and more refined components than necessary, since one of the really hard parts of the job is finding what needs to be done. Initially, hundreds of nice little general-purpose components suggest themselves, but as the library grows, seeing what is needed next becomes increasingly difficult. One does not want to finish any one component development project too quickly, because then you either have to become really creative again, or sit on your hands and risk someone noticing you.

Again looking to the book trade for inspiration and understanding, this can be thought of as the "school textbook" model, in which teams of special-ists try to figure out what should be taught and how, creating books by com-mittee. Often the results are resplendent with splashy color graphics, tables, exercises, and catchy sidebars on every third page. And they're supported by workbooks, teacher's manuals, supplementary readings, and visual aids. They typically are also uninspired, inelegant, even boring, and all too frequently they are hopelessly out of touch with the real needs of schools and students.

Royalties to the author for reuse pose other problems. For one thing, the feedback provided by royalties, whether paid in cash or merely brownie points, generally comes too late. The money has already been spent, not only on com-ponents that see a lot of reuse, but also on ones that proved useless. For any selection process to work, there must be a large pool of parts with substantial variation in "fit" for the selective pressure of the marketplace or environment to work. This means that such libraries will, on the average, always be too big, with a large proportion of mediocre or inferior components from which a small number of "good" ones can be culled. It is hard to know even how the selection process should be driven. Is a widely used component really a desirable one? Perhaps it is so widely used because what is really needed is not in the library. Perhaps its use reflects its position in the index or how it appears in the browser. Perhaps it has simply been better advertised, even though a smaller and more powerful alternative exists.

And what constitutes a use? Each call or instantiation? Each inheritance from or reference to? One program might make 130 uses of a component that is never used in any other project, while another component might find a single use in all 27 systems developed over a year. Which component is more useful? Is a simple and obvious component that becomes widely used worth more royalties to the author than a subtle and ingenious class that saves days of effort on only one project?

Acquired Taste

Of course, other models are possible. Consider the acquisition specialist in a public library whose job it is to track community interests and needs along with industry trends and keep the collection growing appropriately. Like the used-book store, the public library is built from components (books) that are already extant, are acquired intact, and are entered into the library without further editing or refinement.

For a model better suited to building a reusable software component library we need to look further back into publishing, to the actual acquisition of works to be published. Series editors and acquisition specialists in the publishing industry play an active role in seeking out and developing new titles, working with authors not only in response to sensed needs or demands, but also to round out the "book list" for more complete coverage and to anticipate future needs. This model, or Page-Jones's idea of the "art patron" who not only acquires but commissions works, may be closer to what the software industry needs.

Merely assembling *reasonable* components does not make a library of reusable components. We have to get developers to reuse rather than reinvent. Many companies are trying to set up bonus and compensation schemes to reward reuse, but I am not convinced that these are necessary for high levels of productive reuse, and they may even be counterproductive in the long run.

Sometimes information about performance may be all that is needed. In one organization it was enough to change how they reported programming productivity back to the group. Having invested in the development of a reusable component library, they were disappointed with its limited use. They had been posting monthly bar charts showing programmer productivity in lines-of-code written and delivered. They were persuaded to report instead the total number of lines incorporated into delivered code, which included lines linked from the reuse library. Reuse rose sharply. But is lines-of-library-code the right metric for reuse? Correct, reasonable, and appropriate reuse is probably a much more subtle factor, more difficult to define and measure.

Even if we get the right metric, linking the desired behavior of reuse too directly to tangible rewards may create problems. A close link between simple, quantifiable behavior and direct reinforcement, whether in brownie points or quarterly bonuses, can actually undermine the professional values on which effective reuse is based. As workers conform their actions to fit rational reinforcement schemes, underlying values and attitudes about quality work may actually diminish in salience, increasing the dependence on a finely tuned reward structure.

This is why at one of the three-initialed computer companies, their reusability group is focusing on the corporate climate and culture that shapes reuse and reusability, the common values about programs and programming that impede or advance the sharing of designs and implementations. Perhaps I was lucky to be brainwashed by early mentors who thought it was in their best interest and that of our employers not to keep reinventing the wheel. First in nuclear physics data reduction and later in routine business applications, we built and made extensive use of reusable component libraries. These experiences taught me that, with a rich component library supported by effective tools, the rewards are intrinsic. The payoff is finding the component you need in a reasonable time and then finding that it can be readily used or adapted for your use. Every time this happens, you are being reinforced for it. The habit of initially consulting the library or repository becomes ingrained without being tied to increasing the number of green stamps you get or your quarterly code bonus.

Elaborate gimmicks and extrinsic rewards are probably more important for anemic libraries and clumsy tools than for good ones. Perhaps they signal a need to reexamine the corporate culture itself and the professional values it reinforces or discourages.

24

Sputnik Lessons[*]

You've been meaning to learn Smalltalk or to become proficient in Ada or to master the Uniform Object Notation, but there are only so many hours in the day, your client-server project is overdue, and your kids actually would like to see you sometime before they finish high school. Try superlearning! The promos say that you can learn object orientation in an hour. Or a foreign language in three seconds. Superlearning, accelerated learning, multi-sensory education. Powerful new techniques developed by the Russians or the Bulgarians or the Texans. Wouldn't it be great? Slip on some headphones, drift off, and wake up knowing OLE 2.0 and the complete Windows API. Or slip into a lecture, blow your whistle a few times, and walk out thinking objects. Don't you wish?

Today it's sleep-learning and subliminal reprogramming of the unconscious, but it all started with audio training programs, foreign language courses on cassette and, before that, on LPs and even 78s. Which brings me to Sputnik.

Launching Language

Sputnik changed my life. In 1957, the Russians surprised and inspired the world by orbiting the planet's first artificial satellite. This precipitated a change in how Americans viewed space, viewed Russians, and viewed brainy, science-minded

---

[*] From *Software Development*, Volume 1, #11, November 1993.

young people. Until Sputnik, I was an unappreciated misfit. Almost overnight I became an appreciated misfit.

And I decided to learn Russian. There were no classes, so I ordered the newly published, but already obsolescent "Living Language" course on three LPs. The box copy promised quick, easy mastery of a difficult language. Over several months I reached a point where I knew the Cyrillic alphabet and could garble a handful of stock sentences, but I didn't learn Russian. That's hard and takes a lot of time. In fact, it took three consulting trips to Russia before I could get by on the streets of Moscow and Leningrad. Even then, they thought I spoke Russian with a Bulgarian accent.

Learning Smalltalk is certainly easier than learning Russian, but you can't learn either in your sleep. Despite the fact that an entire industry has grown up around it, there is absolutely no credible or consistent evidence that learning can be accelerated by certain forms of music or rhythms or subsonic pulses or that subaudible messages recorded over (or is it under?) New Age music can help you sell systems or lose weight or become more self-confident. None of this stuff is worth the charges on your credit card except to the purveyors of "super" learning.

So how do people learn complex things, like languages or programming languages, or how to program, or how to do therapy? How do they learn to think in terms of procedures or object classes or disabled communication patterns?

Economist Kenneth Boulding, one of the founders of modern systems theory, said that know-how — working knowledge — is not the same as knowledge. Knowledge, even fairly complicated knowledge, can be acquired in many ways, but know-how requires learning-by-doing. You can learn a lot about programming or psychotherapy by reading or watching other people or attending dazzling demos, but you only become a programmer by writing programs or a therapist by doing therapy.

Lectures are probably the least efficient and most ineffective method for teaching. And for obvious reasons they are almost totally useless for imparting know-how. Teachers and trainers should be accountable for how much they successfully communicate, not how much they superficially cover. Droning on over point after point from bullet-laden visuals doesn't communicate a heck of a lot to anyone.

What about multi-media presentations? I was there, on the faculty of IBM's Systems Research Institute when, circa 1970, James Martin first dazzled colleagues and students by using not one but two overhead projectors augmented by 35mm slides. We've come a long way. Now everyone uses two overheads! If you want to lead the pack today, you need a lot more. Color. Sound. Graphics. Animation. Games.

Quick Study

Does multi-media make a difference? Do people learn more or learn faster with color animations? Flashing lights and flashy shirts probably do serve a purpose. At least audiences are more likely to stay awake, which is important, since sleep learning doesn't work. Visible and audible punctuation can help people remember things, but it only works if it is closely, even intrinsically, tied to what it is people are supposed to remember. I remember vividly a spectacular video morph from a lecture over a year ago, but I have no idea what the presenter was talking about. I did like the way the car turned into a hundred-dollar bill, though.

It takes more than bells and whistles to facilitate learning. If there is anything real to be gained from multi-media, multi-sensory communication, it must come from the careful, calculated, and appropriate use of each medium. Back in the heyday of the structural revolution, I worked with a company making multi-media training packages for software development topics. Print, audio, and video media reinforced and complemented each other, because each element in the training was presented in the particular form that conveyed the concepts or skills most effectively.

I spent more than a decade training people in some of the most difficult and complex interpersonal and cognitive skills known: understanding families as working systems and helping families that didn't work too well to work better (Constantine 1986). So I know that you can indeed help people to change how they look at and think about the world, to make what is called, in the current jargon, a paradigm shift. It just doesn't happen in an hour or even a day.

What is the real skinny on this multi-sensory and multi-modality stuff? Learning styles vary. Some people learn better by listening, some by reading, some by seeing. For others, only doing it themselves will work. To some people a picture is worth a thousand words, to others it's only worth seventeen or eighteen. To some very aurally orientated individuals, a graphic or visual may be worthless. Communicating through different sense modalities increases the odds that something you say, show, or do will get through. One sense modality can also reinforce learning in another modality.

Memories for some things are more readily formed or more persistent than others. Scents can lay down highly persistent memory traces after only a single exposure. Spatio-motor learning, the memory for practiced movements and actions, is not only highly persistent but can help in recalling associated thoughts and feelings. Handling things physically, manipulating materials that meaningfully represent ideas, helps to consolidate concepts for learners, but only if the physical manipulations are directly related to the concepts.

Multi-modal communication does not have to involve elaborate multi-media presentations. For example, on a panel at a conference in London I fielded a question from the audience about the relationship between reuse and object technology by holding up two pencils to form a large "L," describing them as orthogonal — independent concepts. Later, relenting under pointed questioning, I acknowledged that the two were somewhat related, that high levels of reuse might be somewhat easier with object technology; I held up the pencils in a broad V, illustrating that they were slightly correlated. Two days later, people were still talking about this mini-demo.

The relationship between reuse and objects is an easy one to demonstrate. The best that good presentation can do is to make easy things easy to learn. Harder things will always be harder. No matter how many senses are engaged, you cannot learn object orientation in an hour any more than you can learn programming in an hour. What you can learn is simplified — some would say watered-down — versions of basic concepts.

25

Up the Waterfall[*]

Do androids dream of electric sheep? Do managers on software projects have nightmares about plunging over waterfalls?

In the traditional view of the software development life cycle, a linear series of stages are completed in sequence, passing from requirements definition through analysis, design, construction, and testing. High-level design is completed before detailed design can be started. Problems are to be thoroughly analyzed and designed before questions about coding are considered. The development process proceeds smoothly from high levels of abstraction to low-level details, from the general and abstract to the specific and concrete.

Of course, it never really works this way. Still, the so-called "waterfall" model of software development continues to be hotly debated. It's a sometimes nightmarish part of our collective mythology. Once you go over a waterfall, your direction and progress are pretty much out of your control. You are going down, whether you like it or not. At best you can hope not to drown. I'll take some of the blame for long ago introducing such over-simplified notions, but, compared to the uncoordinated chaos reigning at the time, even these somewhat simplistic linear life cycle models were progress. Times have not changed all that much.

Getting Ahead

How software engineers and other programming types actually behave is that

[*] From *Software Development*, Volume 2, #1, January 1994

they are constantly getting ahead of themselves. No sooner do they see the title page on the requirements document and they are thinking code or screen layout. When they should be analyzing abstract usage scenarios, they're already thinking about icons for a tool bar. When they should be laying out communications paths through major modules, they start thinking about clever ways to utilize the applications programming interface.

This is normal. In fact, it's part of how normal people normally solve problems. In a sense, they work both ends against the middle, jumping forward and back between ends and means, bouncing up and down from high-level abstraction to low-level details.

But developers aren't supposed to work this way. Getting ahead of yourself in a long and complex project can create real problems. It makes it hard for you and your manager to know how far along the project is. Early commitments to details may later have to be changed, precipitating a cascade of other reworks and work-arounds. Getting into specific details too soon can also distract from the main work at hand.

Traditionally, developers and project leaders have had two basic options whenever this impulse to skip ahead arises. They could stick to the discipline and overcome the impulse, or they could give in to it and do the dirty deed before getting back on track. Either way has its risks. If you stay with the current task and ignore the distraction, important insights or ideas that could prove useful may be lost or forgotten. If you always go ahead and work on the details or the specifics whenever you think of them, you may never get back to the main thread. When you do, the thrust of your grand design may be lost.

Rationalized Reality

What we really need is a life cycle model that takes advantage of the ways most people actually tend to think and work, but which keeps developers from becoming their own worst enemies. The problem is how to capture just enough information that can be used later without disrupting the flow of the current problem-solving activity.

My boss and I were recently working on the user interface design for a desktop applet, trying hard to act like disciplined software engineers applying a systematic interface design strategy, but we repeatedly tripped over our own tendencies to get ahead of ourselves. We kept getting these great ideas about detailed interface layout and behavior when we were supposed to be identifying abstract scenarios describing user needs.

Determined to be organized and systematic, yet committed to making the most of how we spontaneously work best, we started using "bins" to hold all those great little flashes that kept coming up at the wrong time. First developed for managing meetings, bins are a brilliantly simple tool for group problem solving. A bin is just a place — a flipchart or file or notepad — in which to record things that are not for current discussion or debate but which ultimately need to be considered.

Out of this we ended up devising a new conceptualization of the development life cycle. We call it the "feed-forward/work-back" model. It's a rationalized successor to various sequential development models, including not only the waterfall model but also so-called whirlpool models that take developers through an iterative spiral of steps. Feed-forward/work-back is actually one of those very small ideas that could make a big difference in how you work. In principle it could be integrated into virtually any software development life cycle model.

Shuttle Buss

It's called "feed-forward/work-back" because of the kinds of loops it inserts into the development process. When you get ahead of yourself, you feed information forward but don't do the work. This is a feed-forward loop. When you discover an oversight or failure from an earlier phase or activity, you do the necessary work immediately. This is a "work-back" loop. Feed ideas forward, work your way back. That's it. Whenever you get ahead of yourself, you make a note to yourself and your teammates to reconsider something when you get to the appropriate point in the process, wherever that is.

Just think of each phase or activity in the software development life cycle as having its own in-box. It doesn't matter what particular life cycle model you are using, how many activities it has, or even whether it is strictly sequential or loops back on itself. For each designated phase or step or activity you create a conceptual container, an "in-bin," to hold things to be looked at and worked on at the appropriate time.

It is important to create an actual record or file of some sort to serve as the in-bin. If you're using informal group methods, put up a sheet of flipchart paper for each phase or activity. If you do something called "Physical Design Validation" in your software development life cycle, have a sheet labeled "Physical Design Validation — In-bin." If you are using document processing or computer-aided software engineering tools, create a file or folder or other document in the system for each of the in-bins.

When you get to a particular phase or activity, you start out by examining the in-bin, looking through it and sorting its contents for action. Some things may have become irrelevant or may have already been decided or dismissed. Ideas that once seemed spot on may now look way off target. Anything that is still valid or salient can now be worked on.

Sometimes distractions from the current thread of development go in the other direction; they concern matters that should have been taken care of earlier. In these cases, it is clearly best to attend immediately to the out-of-sequence issue in order to allow development to proceed safely and smoothly. You don't want a lot of lurking problems or loose threads bollixing up the system. When you find that some requirement is ambiguous, you go back and firm up the requirements. When you find that some architectural issues were left unresolved, you resolve them. When you find that a poor choice was made for file organization, you go back and rework the file design before moving on.

The aim, of course, is to use lots of feed-forward to reduce the amount of work-back.

26

In-Time Delivery[*]

Our Alitalia flight from Boston to Rome departed late, just as we had been told to expect. Nevertheless, it landed in time for us to catch the direct train for Firenze, where we would have a few days to be pleasantly overwhelmed by the art, the food, and the wines of Tuscany before returning to Rome to teach a class on designing more usable software.

Note that I did not say that our plane landed "on time," but rather "in time." It's a subtle distinction in words, but a cultural matter of great import. Arriving at 6:30 for a 6:30 reception is being "on time." Arriving when the line at the bar has diminished and they bring out the hot *hors d'oeuvres* is being "in time." In time means functional timeliness. As for the Italians, it is not that they are incapable of acting with a sense of urgency, as when their pasta is in danger of cooking past the point of *al dente* perfection, it is just that in Italy, as in various other countries around the world, the cultural sense of time is not closely tied to clock time. A little early, a little late — what counts is the results, the outcome. Italy's neighbors to the north, the Swiss, are at the cultural antipode, operating their trains and their lives by schedules that you can set your Swatch by.

Software and applications development can also be understood on this cultural continuum from on-time development — schedule driven and calendar bound — to in-time development that emphasizes reasonable results within sufficient time to be of value to the users. In some settings, outside

---

* From *Software Development*, Volume 2, #7, July 1994.

forces dictate how the clock runs. Some software for federal and state government applications must incorporate specific features by legally mandated dates, but even here, the twin clocks of on-time and in-time development both tick off the passing hours. The new edition of a tax preparation package faces an absolute 15 April deadline, but in the real world, it is not clear whether this means it must ship by early January or the middle of February to meet customer needs on a timely basis. Still, in most all cases today, management insists that software be delivered on time, and the drop-dead deadlines seem to be coming faster than ever under competitive pressures in a down-sized world of programming.

Rapid and Reasonable

As a result, rapid application development has become one of the methodological rages of our business. Development is "time-boxed" to an absolute schedule of progress and delivery. On-time delivery becomes the paramount if not the singular criterion of project success. High-performance "SWAT" teams of top-gun programmers are armed with the latest and best software tools to reduce the product development cycle time. Delivery within some imagined but absolutely determined market window takes precedence over other objectives. When the deadline is reached, whatever you have is what you deliver — bugs and flaws and all.

True, without deadlines and objectives of some kind, some project teams might never deliver, staying locked in analysis paralysis or designing to a fair-thee-well while the technology changes under them, leaving them stranded high and dry on an isle of obsolete systems. For some people, there is nothing like the terror of approaching deadlines to foster teamwork and productivity.

At one software conference I had a chance to witness this rapid development culture in the extreme. Imagine: your boss hands you the specs for a new app as you walk in the door and tells you that you have 40 minutes to demonstrate a working program. Forget models. Forget methods! This is crunch-mode coding, no more, no less.

This was the premise for the "Visual C++ Superbowl" at Software Development '94. A packed auditorium watched as teams of programmers from Microsoft and Borland cut code at warp speed (Symantec didn't show). Richard Hale Shaw of *PC Week* played Donahue while the judges and the audience alternately gasped, laughed, and applauded. It was, in a word, breathtaking, to plagiarize my friend and fellow judge, J. D. Hildebrand of

Windows Tech Journal. I had forgotten how much fun programming could be. Of course, I was not demonstrating my chops on a 12-foot screen in front of 1,100 people, either. Although few programmers face situations as extreme as this, an increasing number of developers find themselves under the gun to produce software faster and faster. In classes and in my consulting, more and more programmers tell me of draconian deadlines and escalating pressure to deliver by schedules that are handed down as if from Olympus. Often they tell me, "We want to test more thoroughly, but we're told to just ship it as-is." Or, "We'd like to do a better user interface, but the boss won't let us." Or, "We have no time to do it right, we barely have time to do it at all."

In truth, rapid development of applications is real, but the deadlines under which it operates often are not. Targeted delivery dates are pulled from thin air by management and marketing people. I remember being told by one team that they had an absolute deadline for delivery within three months and therefore could not spend the time to model customer requirements or fully design the user interface to requirements. Of course, this absolute deadline had already been extended twice in increments of three months!

Just Do It

I started out programming in precisely this atmosphere, developing routine business applications on fixed-price contracts. We didn't need clairvoyance to see that much of the time we were solving the same problems over and over again. It did not take rocket science to conclude that a library of reusable components for basic business data processing operations would make it possible to build systems faster and more cheaply. But management wouldn't let us take the time to program the library. Billable time ruled all. We didn't have the time to build infrastructure, top management argued, we just had to cut code and ship software.

So we went ahead and built the library anyway, creating new components for it in the course of completing other projects. Sure, we sometimes slipped schedules, but then we almost always did. And eventually we had our library and began to demonstrate substantial gains in productivity. In reality, you don't need permission to do your job well. If you know that a project estimate is unrealistic, then cutting corners in analysis and design won't help. One way or another, now or later, you will take the hit. Since fuller understanding of the problem and better design are apt to cut development costs in the long haul, acting *as if* you had the time may often be the best strategy. The long-term cost to software vendors and in-house developers of delivering poor software, inevitably slipping the shipping date anyway, is certainly more than delivering good software even if it is late. As they say, if you don't have time to do it right, when are you going to get the time to do it over?

In-time delivery of decent software is what really matters for both business and professional success over the long haul. Developers should never simply accept unrealistic deadlines as given. To fulfill their true obligations to employers, they need to learn to negotiate deadlines based on trade-offs in scope and quality.

In some cases, even if the boss says just to ship crap, you may have to go ahead and do a good job anyway.

27

Quality by Increments[*]

Whether it's "Total Quality Management," "Continuous Process Improvement," or ISO-9000, most current notions of process and product quality emphasize enterprise-wide commitment to quality with heavy investment for long-term payoffs. Elaborate schemes for assessing and increasing "process maturity," such as the well-known Capability Maturity Model of the Software Engineering Institute, may have big payoffs, but they can also require a major commitment of resources just to get started (Humphrey, Snyder, Willis 1991) and may have unintended consequences (Bollinger and McGowan 1991). For the greatest, most enduring gains, substantial restructuring and comprehensive quality assurance programs may be necessary, but there are also small, practical steps that can be taken to yield immediate and substantial payoffs in terms of improved software quality and project performance.

Modest changes in how work is organized and carried out can dramatically affect quality in software development. These approaches are not based on technology; they do not involve computer-aided software engineering, object-oriented repositories, new life-cycle methodologies, expert systems for software metrics, statistical quality control, or any of a myriad of other allegedly advanced technical fixes. These steps all go back to basics, to the basic fact that even in high technology it is people who do the work. These approaches have in common that they look to how people and work are organized and managed. Most of these are things that can be put into practice

[*] Revised from *American Programmer*, February 1992.

almost immediately without large investments in training, tools, or inspirational posters.

Setting Priorities

First steps are often the most important, and the first step to improving quality is getting priorities straight. To improve quality in a product and the process by which it is created, quality has to be a priority. If quality is not important to you and to an organization, and it doesn't show in what management actually does and how they do it, quality won't be important to the software development staff. This does not mean posters that declare "Quality Is Job One!" or memos urging employees to strive for zero defects in software. In this area, what counts is how you walk the walk, not how you talk the talk.

- *Make quality important.*

Unfortunately, common assumptions and practices of modern managers often prevent them from making quality a real priority. One major hindrance is that many companies are dominated by the issue of time-to-market. Especially in high-technology fields like software development, management vision is limited, transfixed, unable to see beyond the so-called "market window." If you miss this window of opportunity, so the accepted line of thought goes, all is lost. The idea is to get into the market before anyone else, even if it means shipping a bug-ridden, inferior product. When concern for the market window takes precedence over quality, quality will suffer. It's as simple as that. Timeliness does matter, of course, but it's a matter of priorities. When the choice comes down to packaging and selling what is really a beta-test version now or holding on tight through another round of testing and refinement, which path is followed?

Many software developers continue to let the idea of market window drive their thinking and keep them from producing higher quality systems. Yet the history of our industry is littered with the ghosts of companies that were first in the market and are no more, as well as with innovative but immature products that lost out to later improvements.

- *Look beyond the market window.*

Another way that contemporary management thinking works against making quality a priority is that most companies, especially in the United States, seem more concerned with costs and cost-cutting than with return-on-investment. This is all too easy to do when the economy sours and profits are squeezed. Education, training, and staff development, all recognized as important contributors to quality, are considered to be costs, not analyzed as investments. Staff attendance at conferences and seminars may be an essential part of maintaining a competitive edge, but this is regarded as part of over-head expenses and is often among the first targets of cost cutting.

This is not a matter of soft-headed notions of "being nice" to staff, but a question of the financial basis of management thinking and decision making and how this affects the ability to improving quality. If the cost of a six-month delay in announcing and releasing a product will be paid off in another six months, then rushing to market is not a cost savings.

How money is spent ought to be justified, but the analysis should be based not on cost alone, which is only one side of the equation, but on return on investment. Australian consultant Rob Thomsett has shown, for example, that similar gains can be achieved through investing in CASE technology or in team building, but the return on investment with team building is an order of magnitude better. Still, CASE is flashy technology that can be shown to visitors, while effective teamwork is invisible, so many companies would rather spend on hardware and software than on peopleware.

•   *Think return-on-investment, not cost containment.*

Rewards and Recognition

For quality to be a priority, people must be evaluated and rewarded for turning out quality work. But what do we reward? In software development, productivity, whether in function points or lines of code, is usually what gets the bonus or promotion or recognition, if anything. Or we reward herculean, last-ditch efforts to meet seemingly impossible deadlines. Ironically, in many companies it is in the best interests of project managers to ensure that all-out efforts are needed toward the end of a project. Such highly visible commitments are what is most likely to win approval whether the project succeeds or not. "Well, we lost the contract, but no one can fault Pete, who worked around the clock right up to the deadline."

The problem is not that people don't care about quality, as some managers complain. One study of 11,000 people in six industries (by Brooks International in 1991) found that more than nine out of ten employees felt a personal responsibility for doing quality work. But seven out of ten reported that quality was not an important factor in how their work was evaluated. And a bare one out of four said that their management really rewarded improvements in quality. What do we reward, then? The truth is, recognition and rewards of any kind are a lot less frequent than most managers think. Some 80% of managers claim they give their subordinates sincere and thorough praise, but only one out of seven of their subordinates see it that way (Lickert 1989).

If we want to improve quality, we ought to follow the Ferber Principle. Psychiatrist Andrew Ferber was once asked what was the most important thing for beginning therapists to know if they wanted to help client families improve. His answer:

- *Whenever you see something you like, applaud like crazy.*

Measurement and Control

Nearly everyone has heard the dictum that you can't control what you can't measure (DeMarco 1982). This is often a prelude to a hard sell on starting a software metrics or statistical quality control program. Formal measures have many advantages, but a moment's reflection will tell you that there are many important things in life that parents, teachers, managers, and others control but that they do not measure. Many of these probably cannot be measured. When it comes to people, the essential thing is attention, not measurement; what matters is what you monitor. Any effective parent knows that if you pay attention to tantrums you get more tantrums. Systems in general, and human systems in particular, have the peculiar property that the very act of observation changes what is being observed. This is the basis of the well-established Hawthorne effect: simply making a group the object of study, paying more attention to what they are doing, can lead to improved performance.

- *Pay attention.*

What, in particular, you monitor matters, of course, because whatever you monitor is affected. If programmers are evaluated on the tightness of their code, they produce smaller systems; if user friendliness is the criteria, you get friendlier programs (Weinberg and Schulman 1974).

In Australia, the new manager of a maintenance programming group wanted to improve not only the effectiveness of his team, but also its status and recognition in the company. Among other things, he started sending reports back to the original programmers about the bugs discovered and corrected in their systems after they were "in production." A programmer might get a note simply saying that over the weekend the system had crashed without closing the output file, but that Maintenance Programmer Quinnthorpe had tracked it to a loop in module Z091, which was corrected, recompiled, and tested in 1.6 hours.

An interesting thing happened as the result of this practice. The new systems being put into production got more reliable and started passing acceptance tests more quickly. The mere act of monitoring quality and reporting the results can bring it under control and improve it.

- *Give feedback.*

In another company, bar charts were posted every month showing programmer productivity in lines of code written and debugged. After the reports were changed to include all delivered code, not only that written by programmers but also all included modules from the reusable component library, reuse rose dramatically (see Chapter 23).

Feedback is the essential ingredient. When workers have access to information about their performance and its relationship to organizational objectives, quality goes up. This is the basis of the open-book model of management, in which workers are given not only reports about production and defects, but financial information about related costs, revenues, and profits (Case 1990; Finegan 1990). With this kind of information in hand, workers are in a better position to optimize how they spend their time and to improve their own work process. The key is feedback that ties individual and team performance to the larger financial picture, for example, reporting not only programming time and program defects, but the costs of these and the resulting profit (or loss) on a project. Many managers have learned that it's a two-way street. When more information is shared with staff, they share more with management, and a continuous flow of ideas for improvement results. In technical management, we tend to think of measurement mostly in terms of numbers with three-digit precision or better. But qualitative methods and measures or simple rankings may often be enough to evaluate and bring a process under control. The theory of measurement, a part of statistics, recognizes various levels of measurement. Numbers that you can multiply and divide are at one level, a so-called ratio scale, those you can add and subtract at another, lower level, called interval scaling. But even where results can only be quantified enough to say that one thing is better than another by some unknown amount, statistical analyses are possible.

You do not need to measure altitude to the nearest meter to find the lookout tower at the top of the mountain. All you need to know is whether each step is taking you down or up. For many processes, effective strategies for improvement can be based on measurement as crude as just knowing whether you are getting better or worse.

Data and Information

Most managers would probably claim to value information and would like to think that they base their decisions on data. Unfortunately, these same managers often keep themselves from getting the information they need and may be oblivious to some of the information they do have.

The true scientist knows that there is no such thing as an experiment that fails. Whatever happens yields information that can lead to revising the hypothesis or refining the technique. In family therapy training I learned that whatever happens in a session is informative, or, as we used to tell our trainees:

- *Remember, it's all data.*

The true manager knows that all news is good news. Information about a process has intrinsic value and should be valued. How you react to information affects how accessible it will be in the future. Where one side is rewarded, the truth will not be known. The problem with punishing the bearer of bad news is not only that it's hell on messengers but eventually it assures that only good news will reach you. The "bad" news, which is often the most critical to know about, isn't delivered.

I once had a boss who told me that he would never hold it against me for keeping him informed of problems, that he particularly wanted to be kept apprised of difficulties that might jeopardize the agency we both worked for. He not only kept his word, but also left the resolution of such problems to me and my staff. This helped keep the lines of communication open and insured that he had access to information critical to his decision making.

In improving any process, the most important information to know, of course, is about problems and failures, yet this is precisely the information that managers may be warding off. Finding a bug in a program ought to be the occasion for a celebration. In fact, all program faults should be not only recorded, but also studied.

- *Record and study defects.*

Keeping detailed logs of all problems — defects and mistakes, customer complaints, design changes, analysis errors, "improvements" in beta testing — is one essential step. The other is to study these systematically and periodically. This means setting aside as part of every project the time for systematic reflection. If we don't study and learn from our mistakes, how can we avoid them in the future?

To improve quality, it is especially important that we never confuse opposition or criticism with disloyalty.

- *Encourage criticism.*

It is often the contrary view or the critical perspective that offers the most information about potential improvements to the process. In fact, the quality of problem solving is critically dependent on critical input. Groups that include a "resident critic" or "devil's advocate," or that exploit dialectical processes of opposing ideas and active critique, perform better (Constantine 1989; Priem and Price 1991).

Of course, it is not simply enough to know that something is wrong or even how it is going wrong; we have to do something about it. Program bugs are not just information about something wrong in specific programs; they are also information about problems in the process that generated the programs. The first question is how did it get there? The goal is not to fix blame, but to learn how to change the process so that it is less likely to happen in the future. Organizations that continually improve their processes take each failure as an occasion to retrain or to refine the process and improve it.

- *Correct the process, not just the program.*

Work Visibility

A powerful principle of quality improvement is found in the title of a hit song from the 1960s:

- *Let the sun shine in.*

Invisibility is the enemy of quality. We can't improve what we don't see. One of the best ways to assure that somebody sees a problem is to make what software developers are doing more visible.

Experience has shown that the quality of software can be markedly improved simply by increasing the amount of work that is done face-to-face (Chapter 22). When two or more people work together on the same problem, quality goes up. On the average, increasing the visibility of work increases quality. Why? Basically, in order for two programmers cutting code together to introduce a bug or a departure from standards and practices, they have to collude; to find the bug or spot the departure, only one has to see it. Forget about what you've heard about "groupthink" or collective mediocrity. It turns out that such effects exist but depend on special conditions. Group leaders can do simple things that go a long way toward improving the quality of problem solving and avoiding groupthink. Simply by delaying or withholding their own opinions, group leaders can significantly improve the problem solving of any group (Anderson and Balzer 1991).

The "two-to-a-terminal" model of programming, which I have called the "Dynamic Duo," dates from the era that introduced "ego-less programming." Ego-less programming was based on the notion that programmers had too much ego invested in their code. If only they could work in an ego-less style, becoming less defensive and more open to the review, suggestions, and criticisms of others, they would produce better code. There were a number of problems with this way of thinking, not the least of which is that people have egos. Modern management thinking, rather than trying to stamp out or overcome egos, seeks to take this reality of human nature into account and turn it to the collective good.

The watchword today is "ownership" or "buy-in." Progressive organizations seek to increase the sense of personal ownership — ego investment, if you will — that employees have in the products of their efforts. For example, the structured open model for teamwork (see Chapter 16) is an approach to organizing project teams that uses consensus-based problem solving to increase work visibility and individual ownership.

An essential variant on the theme of work visibility is the idea of separation of powers. It's implicit in the Dynamic Duo approach to programming. While one programmer is at the keyboard, the other is looking over his shoulder. The programmer at the keyboard has one set of responsibilities associated with defining the algorithm and mapping out the flow in code. The other is looking for the holes in the logic, trying to spot weaknesses or errors.

- *Separate powers.*

This principle is an essential component of "cleanroom" programming, an approach that has produced some moderate to large-scale systems demonstrated to be virtually bug-free (Cobb and Mills 1990). In this model, one person or group writes the code, trying to "get it right." But someone else compiles and tests it, trying to find what is wrong with it. There is more to the model, but simply this kind of separation of responsibilities in itself seems to improve quality. Knowing that someone else on the team is not only going to see the code, but take over compiling and testing, seems to lead to greater care and more effort to get it right the first time.

Skills and Stars

Decades of research and practical experience has taught us that often more than an order of magnitude in productivity separates the best programmers from the worst, and the best are typically twice as productive as the average ones (De-Marco and Lister 1987). Some groups have dramatically improved quality and productivity by the simple expedient of cutting their programming staff, keeping only the best half. One approach to quality is to take only the very best players, give them all the resources and motivation they need to do the best job, and let them do it. This may be especially appealing in an era of "downsizing."

- *Use only the finest ingredients.*

Of course, every manager knows that there are "stars" in any organization, but not everyone wants to get rid of all the supporting players. What we'd really like to do is find a way to help the others "get better." Which brings us to the principle of cross-training. The idea is to create more opportunities for software development people to learn from each other.

- *Let each one teach one.*

One of the most effective and efficient ways to accomplish this cross-training is to build it into the way projects are organized. This goes back to work visibility. By doing more of their work in face-to-face groups, team members automatically learn more from each other. In addition, rotating responsibilities as a normal part of software development gives opportunities to practice, helping to gradually disperse skills and knowledge through the group.

Differences in natural talent and achievable levels of skill will always persist. Some programmers will always be better at cutting clever code, some better at modeling essential abstractions; one team member might always be a better group facilitator than the others. But in an organization that encourages and makes room for cross-training and skill dispersion, the average level of skill in any of these areas is always increasing. Over time, people will pick up more and more of each other's specialties. They will never reach the point where everyone can do all the jobs with equal skill, but the differences will diminish. Most importantly, team members become increasingly able to fill in for each other. The organization as a whole becomes less critically dependent on the skills and presence of any one member. An entire project need not then become stalled simply because one person becomes ill or takes a job in another city.

Degrees of Freedom

Ironically, in many organizations that sincerely want to improve quality, common practices create conditions preventing improvement. Things as simple as how deadlines and budgets are established can make or break a project in terms of quality. In the typical situation, all factors — budget, allocation of resources, staffing, methodology, and deadline — are fixed when the project is given to software developers. Where can we get improved quality? We need at least one degree of freedom. If all the variables are constrained, the system is over-determined and there is no way to win. So what is sacrificed when there are problems? Quality! Under tight deadlines, such as those driven by some imagined market window, it often comes down to, "We don't have time to do it right." This points to one of the simplest changes that has been found to help improve the quality of software.

*   *Negotiate deadlines.*

    Software developers need to be directly involved in establishing delivery dates and project deadlines. Setting a completion target should be approached as a negotiation in which there are recognized trade-offs. "Yes, the project can be delivered by the end of the year if you don't mind having a defect rate around 15 per KLOC. Or we can promise a lower defect rate if you don't mind cutting out half the screens."

Summary

Approaches to raising software quality do not have to be complicated or involve large budgets. Some simple things can make a big difference. First, get your priorities straight, make quality a priority. Don't let the market window run your business. Think in terms of return-on-investment, not cost containment.

Then, pay attention, recognize and reward quality. Give feedback, and be generous with information. Keep listening: remember that all news is good news, especially bad news. Encourage critical feedback. Record and study defects, and correct the process, not just the program. Let the sun shine in; make work more visible. Promote cross-training: let each one teach one. When quality is especially essential, use only the finest ingredients. And always negotiate your deadlines!

VI

Software Usability

Introduction

The user interface is the point of contact between programs and people, the river that marks the boundary between the user and the used. Software developers stand on both sides of this river. As programmers they are, in a sense, inside the computer, where they see the usual mess or the exceptional elegance of the actual code that makes things happen. At the same time they are users of computer software, outsiders looking in, seeing not the code but the arrangement of features and fields that make their development tools and support systems either more or less usable. They have, therefore, a double interest in the user interface: as designers and as users.

Usability is arguably the essential measure of software quality. It does not matter much whether a program has spectacular graphics or speedy algorithms or even bug-free performance if it is all but impossible to use. If a system does not do something that is useful, if it does not provide services or capabilities that meet user needs, can it be said to be a good system?

As computers themselves have become more accessible and more people directly and regularly interact with them, matters of usability and user interface design have received growing attention in the software world. The purview of software designers has gradually expanded outward from the internal structures of program and data to the user interface. At first, much of the concern centered on the technology, on the software side of the design. Software developers gradually learned to deal more directly with detailed choices of the devices and mechanisms used to interact with users, along with their arrangement within the user interface. From this concern with the technical details of the user interface the focus then shifted further outward, toward the users themselves. Software and applications developers were admonished to deal with real users, to converse with them more often and in more depth in order to understand their preferences and incorporate their ideas and suggestions, even to bring representative users into the design and development process itself. Programmers who once kept their distance from users except when forced to get their approval on requirements specifications now find themselves dealing with end users in meetings and planning sessions or even as continuing members of the development team.

From this user-centered view we are now seeing some movement toward more focus on uses than users, more emphasis on the intent of users than their preferences. This "teleocentric" or purpose-centered view of systems considers real needs to be more important than wants. The hope is to build software that better supports the work of real people, that serves useful purposes and makes tasks easier or simpler.

Whether this trend will continue and how far it will go is unclear, but here are some of the important issues regarding the user interface, the users, and the uses of software as we now understand them.

Consistency and Conventions[*]

We are surrounded by user interfaces. The term may have gained currency through computer software, but every system and every piece of equipment that has users by definition has a user interface. As psychologist and now Apple Fellow Donald Norman has shown us (Norman 1988), we can learn a great deal about how to design and build better user interfaces for software simply by looking around us, by thinking about how the controls of common appliances, utensils, and tools make it easier or more difficult for us to use them.

Think about the last time you rented a car or borrowed one from somebody. Probably it was a different make or model from the one you usually drive. You slipped into the driver's seat, buckled up, and checked the mirrors. Then you drove off. The question is, how many seconds did it take for you to learn the user interface of this system? Did you attend a training workshop or view a video on how to use this particular car? Or were you able to figure it out on your own without having to read the manual?

---

[*] From *Computer Language Magazine*, Volume 9, #11, November 1992.

The user interface of most of today's automobiles, with a few annoying exceptions, conform to the Great Law of Usability (Constantine 1991b). This law states that the user interface should enable a user who has expertise in the application domain to use the system without training and without reference to a manual or other instructions outside of the system. In other words, a good user interface allows users who already know what they are doing to just go ahead and do it without having to learn something new.

Know-how

Of course, you already knew how to drive. You probably qualify as an expert automobile user — not necessarily a professional, but fully qualified and trained. For the expert, driving becomes what psychologists call an over-learned skill. You can do it without giving it much conscious attention. Consider this remarkable little experiment the next time you are driving and talking with a passenger. As you are talking, let yourself become aware of the fact that you are also driving. How is this happening? Driving is a very complex information processing task, as a team of Army scientists and engineers learned when they tried to program a computer to drive a van. And even an ordinary casual conversation is far more complex than driving a car. Yet experienced drivers can attend to the thread of the conversation and relegate most of the problems of driving to background processing using stable subroutines.

When you slipped behind the wheel of that unfamiliar automobile, you were aided in adjusting to the new user interface by two things. It probably fit quite closely with the way in which you "naturally" carry on your over-trained dialogue with a car, and it was probably not dramatically different from the one in your own car. The instrument panel and controls of most cars follow a few basic conventions. Gear shifts are either on the steering column or on the floor between driver and passenger, the speedometer is typically dead ahead on the dash board, the steering wheel is round, and the turn signal, to the left on the steering column except in countries where you drive on the left side of the road, is tilted clockwise for a right turn, counter-clockwise for left, just like the steering wheel. The interface is both consistent with established conventions and internally consistent. Now and then you encounter something odd and have to play around a bit to figure out how to get the headlights on, but even this is likely to take only a few moments.

It surprises many people to learn that almost none of the standard user interface features of an ordinary passenger car are regulated by state or federally mandated standards. The law does not even require a steering wheel or even that it be round. Some special cars are indeed built with alternative steering devices for special classes of users. Some years ago, a German automotive company got cute with an oval steering wheel on one of its sporty models, but drivers hated it. The steering wheel is the way it is because long experience has shown that rotation of a round wheel is both a good metaphor and an efficient mechanism for controlling direction of travel.

Rising Standards

It was not always thus. In the early days of the evolution of the automobile, numerous other controls for steering were tried. Tiller bars were common in early models, in part because the actual mechanics were simpler. But steering wheels eventually won through a process of natural selection among engineers and the driving public. This evolution was possible precisely because automotive designers were not constrained by premature standards nor were they compelled to be different for the sake of being different simply because someone or some company claimed intellectual property rights on the "look-and-feel" of circular steering controls.

For most of the really important aspects of user interfaces, standards are unnecessary. Superior arrangements and mechanisms will gradually win out in the marketplace of products and of ideas. Tiller bars, like steering wheels, establish a fairly simple translation between control movement and directional change, but they have critical limitations. If a group of well-intentioned industry leaders or a government standards body had mandated a standard "look-and-feel" for steering controls when tiller bars had the lead, automobiles would have been kept limited to local travel at modest speeds.

The First Law of Conventions was aptly stated by K. D. Mackenzie a quarter century ago (Mackenzie 1966). When there is more than one way to do something and the choice among alternatives is essentially arbitrary, pick some one way and *always* do it that way. When the choice among alternatives is not arbitrary, it is important to pick a good one.

P. J. Plauger, who is both sufficiently principled and sufficiently masochistic to devote substantial time to international standards efforts, talks of the Principle of Good Enough (Plauger 1993). A standard for information interchange or for a programming language or for telephone interfaces does not have to be ideal or perfect, it does not even have to be "right." In practice, ideal standards are politically and technically impossible, anyway. All that is needed is that a standard be "good enough." As a rule, human cleverness and evolving technology will overcome most limitations or shortcomings anyway.

The question is, just what is "good enough" when it comes to such widely used facilities as graphical user interfaces? The most important kind of consistency is consistency with the way people think and work when they are not forced to do things the way some software system does. The human cerebral cortex has remarkable plasticity. People learn. They can adjust to amazingly difficult interfaces, but there is always a cost.

Most of what people know and do has nothing to do with computers. (Sorry programmers, but that's the harsh reality!) Although some things are hard-wired into the human brain, most things people claim as intuitive are really conditioned. In fact, psychologists now define intuition in terms of complex associations and processing that have been learned so well they are no longer fully conscious activities.

Counterintelligence

When you force users to interact with a system in a way that counters those conventions that have already been programmed in through experience or wired in through evolution, you increase frustration and fatigue, and you build in an added, permanent increase in errors. Even small increases in the probability of error due to the user interface can be significant. Consider even a tiny increase in errors in the data entry processes for today's gigabyte databases. Or consider the consequences of such effects due to problems in the interfaces of the software development tools by which computer software is itself designed and created.

Unfortunately, most current graphical user interfaces are just not good enough. They are inconsistent, unnecessarily complex, and full of conventions that are seriously and demonstrably wrong. Microsoft's public admission that Windows might not be a perfectly suitable basis for control of household appliances and other consumer products is monumental understatement. The problems are not in details of style that might be tweaked into suitability, but are fundamental flaws in the most basic mechanisms.

To pick but one example, consider scroll bars as the mechanism and metaphor for controlling movement of a drawing or writing surface in relation to a smaller "window" through which only a portion can be viewed. Scroll bars are to on-screen navigation what tiller bars are to automotive navigation (Constantine 1994d)! They slow and limit the user, giving feedback that can be misleading and confusing, leading to wasted moves, increased errors, and disruption of thought processes. They require the user to move in a way that runs absolutely counter to how the brain works. To move left or right, you have to first move down, to move up or down, you start by moving to the right.

To understand how problematic a simple but counter-intuitive interface can be, do this little experiment. Turn your mouse one quarter turn counter-clockwise and then try positioning the on-screen cursor. This spatial transformation seems simple, but is almost impossible to get the hang of.

Outside of the world of computers are systems and applications that must solve similar problems of navigation through panning, scrolling, and zooming. Two that are worth thinking about as a source of ideas for graphical user interfaces are microfiche readers and video cameras. Among the dozens of mechanisms for controlling on-screen navigation that have been designed, including by the author, are any number that are demonstrably and dramatically better than scroll bars (Constantine 1994d). If you don't think this could make a difference in real work, considers how many times a day you or your customers pan and scroll your way around documents, diagrams, and displays.

Calls for standardization in graphical user interfaces may be a bad idea that seems good at the time. The question is whether you want to be stuck forever driving your computer with a tiller bar.

29

Complexity and Creeping Featurism*

I hate moving. I hate upgrading software. I hate the transition to a new machine. In principle, migrating to the next platform or version is simple and efficient; in practice, it throws my normally somewhat disheveled everyday existence into extended and unfathomable chaos. Most of all, however, I hate learning a new word processor.

As a purveyor of ideas, the two pieces of software closest to me are my graphics package and my word processor. These tools are my constant companions. I want them to be nice to me and to get along with each other. They define the limits of what I can do in expressing myself in words and pictures, and they put ceilings on my productivity. They enable me to leap tall in-boxes in a single bound, or they trip me up on trivial tasks. As with underwear or deodorant, my preferences for certain of these tools over others is deeply personal, fierce, and irrational.

I originally migrated to Windows because the graphics package that I needed (or was it wanted?) ran under Windows. Migration connotes some sort of steady progress, but this felt more like defenestration. Having taken the plunge, I was faced with the annoyance of switch hitting between my word processor and a suite of tools under DOS and my drawing tool under Windows. Like palindromic arthritis, this is not crippling, but it is a constant pain.

* From *Computer Language Magazine*, Volume 9, #10, October 1992.

In the interest of smoother collaboration with a growing cadre of colleagues who all used the same Windows/Macintosh word processor, I accepted one of those come-on offers to upgrade. To appreciate the aptness of the term "upgrade," picture a grade that goes up — steeply!

I am not saying this word processor was not user friendly. It has more cute buttons than a professional seamstress and more files of context-sensitive help than your high school guidance counselor. Using the handful of simple everyday operations is no big deal. In fact, it probably does almost anything I would ever want it to do, but finding where all those handy things were hiding, especially those treasures that spell the difference between meeting and missing a deadline, took many months.

Progress

Despite the fact that most major word processors are now in version numbers ranging from 5.0 to 7.0, they have not become easier to learn. The ads make that claim, but what they really mean is that it takes less time to get started. Almost anyone can begin doing useful work within minutes of completing the installation. After that you hit the wall. The best of today's word processors is significantly harder to really learn — to master — than the early systems on CP/M or Apples. Here we are, several generations down the pike from such forgotten gems as Electric Pencil and Spellbinder, and the tools, though much more powerful, are in many ways also more unwieldy.

Part of the problem is that simple, early text processors evolved into word processors, primarily by doing more; then word processors were transmuted into "word publishers" with still more capability. Now, high-end systems, such as WordPerfect and Word for Windows, are becoming almost indistinguishable from full-blown desktop publishing software in terms of what you can do with them, even if they operate in somewhat different ways. They are crammed chock-a-block with bells and whistles, and it takes a slew of hooks and handles to get them to ring and toot in the right places and at the right times.

Word processors, and a growing legion of our most important software tools, have become victims of creeping featurism, a serious malady of user interfaces that strikes software in its prime and can, if left unchecked, cripple the user. Untreated, creeping featurism can leave users with an agoraphobic response to large, open dialogue boxes, or even with a lingering fear of unknown menus. Sometimes the clearest sign is a vaguely anxious feeling that somewhere, lurking in some unexpected cascade of pull-down menus, is that wonderful shortcut that resided on Ctrl-Alt-F5 within your last system.

Selling Points

Features sell. Software reviewers stress features and highlight them in neat comparison tables packed with check marks and dashes or circles of various shades. Vendor advertisements vie for the most bullets on the function list. Consumers learn to discriminate at a glance between a "full-featured" personal information manager and one with only limited functionality. Most buyers will never use more than a small fraction of all those options and operations, but it's a comfort just knowing that they are there against some unlikely and unanticipated need. After all, more is better, right?

Creeping featurism is a chronic degenerative disease. The syndrome is defined not by the number of features but by how they are acquired and by how they are embodied in the software and presented to the user. Creeping featurism results from the slow accretion of capabilities and is reflected in a bumpy and irregular user interface marred by idiosyncrasies and special functions that seem to grow like warts or carbuncles in the oddest places.

Creeping featurism is debilitating because when you add a new feature you have to put it someplace. In an extant system it is quite possible that none of the available places to put things make much sense. If nonprinting comments were not in the early versions of the word processor and were not planned for in the original interface layout, the function for creating and editing them may just have to be stuck somewhere stupid, like on the function key for importing and exporting DOS text files, to pick one unlikely but real example.

Creeping featurism often results in scattering related operations or options in different parts of the user interface. After four or five rounds of revision, the dozens of "tack ons" and "work arounds" lead to a user interface covered with little appendages, oddments of switches, and addenda to menus. With time, the shape of the interface more and more reflects the internal dictates of program constraints and organization: how the programmers had to think of the functions in order to find places to hang them. Old timers, with calloused thumbs and bent fingers from years of wrapping their hands around these features, get so used to them that they hardly think twice when they key in Ctrl-F5-C-C. Continuing to support these reprobates commits vendors to still more interface barbarism, since new features must not interfere with the controls for these old ones.

What the user really wants (or is it needs?) is a simple interface to control these complex systems. Unfortunately, today's software is too often only simple on the surface and gets messy as soon as you try to do any real work with it. Of course, by then, you are out of the software store and bound by the shrink-wrap agreement.

Humans deal with complexity by chunking, by lumping together similar or related things into chunks that can be tossed around mentally as a single unit. Really good user interfaces do the same thing, by reducing to a minimum the total number of distinct ideas or techniques the user must learn. This takes careful thought in the first place and regular reworkings to overcome the messiness introduced by creeping featurism.

For example, from the standpoint of a person using a word processor, straight lines are lines are lines. The user wants to draw a line and put it somewhere. Whether it runs down the margin to "redline" text, or separates text body from footnotes, or boxes in a table, or frames a sidebar comment, or is a 3-point rule in a snazzy letterhead, it's just a line. It looks like a line when we print it out, and we call it a line when we tell a co-worker to "get rid of that line down the side." Yet most word processors treat each variant as a separate and unrelated phenomenon.

My old word processor had two basic ways to draw lines, or rules, as typesetters say. This split interface was based not on any external user considerations but really on internal implementation details. The older, more primitive feature used line drawing text characters. The newer, more versatile way used graphics. In an ironic twist, the old way was semi-WYSIWYG — you drew under control of the cursor keys and could see what the results would be as you created them. The new way required entering choices and values for the type of line, position, and weight. Even after you finished, you couldn't see what you did without going into a print preview mode, a legacy of the old DOS text-based restrictions.

But now consider my next word processor! It has five completely different ways to create lines. These are indexed separately in the manual and accessed through different menus or buttons in the software. Some lines you can get rid of by pointing at and pressing delete, some you can't. Obviously, creeping featurism has struck again. The end result is more complexity than is necessary and the appearance of more complexity than there is.

Darwinian Design

I am certainly a firm believer in evolution, in malleable software designs that are steadily reworked to conform to the user in response to an ever deepening understanding of what it is we are trying to do with our tools and how the tools can best help us. On the down side, the evolutionary process in software engineering can result in a patchwork of parts and pieces that may work but that punishes the user. After two or three integer version releases, the entire user interface should probably be redesigned from scratch to cover the same functionality with a fraction of the controls.

In the meantime, I had to paw through the thicket of creeping features to figure out how to make a simple 3-point rule from margin to margin with my wonderful(?) new Windows word processor. I was sure it was in there, somewhere, but it took awhile to track it down amidst the zits and pimples on the user interface.

30

Going to the Source[*]

What do users want, anyway? And how do you find out? Software developers are being told to produce the systems their clients and customers want, to become more user-oriented. Companies in every field are trying to be more competitive by listening to "the voice of the customer" and becoming "customer-driven." It is not enough anymore to have software with the right features. The software needs to have a good user interface: to be easy to learn and easy to use. But how do you know what users want in a user interface, anyway? Many companies turn to market research, to telephone and written surveys that ask users or potential users what they want.

Sometimes it appears they don't even know themselves, and often it seems that what they want may not be at all what they need. A major developer of accounting software accumulated over 15,000 requests and suggestions for changes from its customers between one integer release and the next. Many of these were patently ridiculous, and careful study showed that others would have been mistakes to incorporate into the software.

Wishing Well

In folk tales, peasants who are granted three wishes invariably seem to call disaster down on their village. If you ask users directly what they want, they will typically ask for more features. If you simply respond like some obedient software

[*] From *Computer Language Magazine*, Volume 9, #12, December 1992.

genie, you will unleash another epidemic of creeping featurism (Chapter 29). Worse, the surveyed users may not have a clue what to ask for, but flattered by the attention and taken by the sense of responsibility, they will just make something up. Then the real trouble starts.

To the user, the user interface *is* the system. To find out what is needed or what is right and wrong with a given system, you do need to go to the source. If you don't ask, you probably aren't going to find out. Developers who rely on their own expertise or judgment alone, or who trust spontaneous feedback and complaints from customers, put themselves at a competitive disadvantage.

User surveys are an obvious tool, but the truth is that most users just won't take the time to respond to questionnaires, and those who do often do so casually, with little attention to needed detail. Telephone surveys or in-person interviews are likely to get a little more information from users than if you make them do the work of writing things down, but all surveys suffer from problems of recall. I remember there were confusing things with the 3-D features of my new graphics package, but now that I've learned how to use them, I can't recall just what confused me at first. The essential information for the developers is already lost, namely, the exact point when I hit the wrong button or got results that didn't look like what I expected.

For most software developers, beta test sites are a major source of feedback. Especially if a company establishes a close working relationship with a number of good sites, valuable information can be obtained this way. However, there are also serious limitations to beta testing for interface design and refinement.

In particular, if a product is fairly flaky or is still quite rough around the edges, a customer may run into literally hundreds of small glitches or minor difficulties in a single day of typical use. Trying to make note of all these as they arise interrupts the flow of work so badly that all but the most dedicated and compulsive beta testers end up recording only a fraction of the problems they actually encounter. Equipping users with a voice-operated tape recorder increases the capture rate, but this, too, tends to interfere with normal patterns of work.

To get around these limitations, it is becoming fashionable for major software companies to build usability labs or usability research centers. These facilities use both audio and video recording and are usually fitted with one-way mirrors for observing systems in use. The centers are typically equipped with a range of computers and workstations.

Aside from the cost of setting up and operating such a research facility, a major shortcoming is that people do not behave in the laboratory like they do when they are on their own turf. If you want to know how people work with a particular piece of software, you need to study them *in context*, using some form of contextual inquiry, such as the approach pioneered by Karen Holtzblatt and her colleagues at Digital Equipment Corporation (Holtzblatt and Beyer 1993).

The essence of a contextual approach is to investigate what users do when they are doing their usual job in the usual setting. It's like the field research that a cultural anthropologist or ethnographer would undertake. People are observed in their work and informants are interviewed about how work is carried out. A skilled interviewer can elicit remarkably detailed information about actual usage with minimal interference in the work process.

Of course, to actually watch a person using a system, there must be a system to be used. Prototypes are often employed in early phases of development, alpha and beta versions later. A really good field researcher can sometimes get useful data from nothing more than paper prototypes, simple static drawings of proposed screen layouts.

You can also get ideas for new tools and features by seeing what people do with the tools they already have, where giving them something just a little different could significantly simplify work flow, for example. You might also give them your competitor's software and learn what is wrong with it. Or you can even study how they do their jobs in the absence of a software tool. The idea isn't simply to automate the manual process, but to learn how and where software support can actually help.

Office Visits

The central idea of contextual methods is to get out of *your* office and interact with users in *their* offices. Not only does this give you better data on which to base your design decisions, it costs less. Building a half-million-dollar usability research facility may get you written up in the trade rags and may signal the marketplace that, by golly, your company is truly committed to better user interfaces and to client-centered design, but hopping into your car with a notebook and a tape recorder may lead to better software.

On the down side, most people do not particularly cotton to having someone looking over their shoulders as they try to do their jobs. And, being watched changes how they do it. When an interface designer or usability investigator sits at the user's elbow taking notes, an interaction is set up that changes what the user does. The designer gives the user unconscious cues: a sudden intake of breath, a quick scribble on the pad, a quiet "ah" or "hmmm," leaning back or leaning forward, shifting in the chair restlessly. In myriad ways subtle messages are communicated about what the user is doing or ought to be doing instead of the incredibly stupid moves being made. The temptations to "help" are great, and typical developers just love to step in and take over when someone else is making less than optimal use of "their" software. Untrained or inexperienced investigators often make even more blatant interventions. ("Here, let me show you an easier way." "Ah, just click there." "No, not quite.")

It works the other way, too. The user knows you are there watching. They know you understand the system, perhaps better than they do, so they look to you for guidance, whether with outright questions or glimpses over the shoulder.

All in all, it is probably better not to be there. So does this mean just go back to the office and start building that usability lab so you can stay behind the one-way mirror? Not necessarily.

A simple technology works amazingly well. A video camcorder is aimed over the user's shoulder, focused on the keyboard and screen. Beside the screen is an adjustable mirror oriented so the user's face is visible to the camera. That's it.

In a typical investigation, a user is video taped making use of some piece of software. This tape is first reviewed by the investigators to study what the user is doing. Being able to see the user's face gives the investigators additional clues about what is happening. When the user is surprised, annoyed, confused, or impatient, it says volumes about details of the interface.

The investigator then sits down with the user to watch selections from the tape. The idea is to tap into intentions and reactions, what the user was thinking about and actually trying to do while using the software. Here's where the mirror comes into play again. When people see themselves, especially their own faces, on a recording, they can often recall with amazing accuracy and detail their own "inner dialogue" and feelings from the time of the recording session. If you take the trouble to obtain it and understand it, this information can tell you what your users *need.*

In the short run, giving customers what they want — or said they wanted on some market survey — can be a winning strategy, but in the long run it probably pays off more to give them what they really need, especially if you can package it so it looks like what they wanted or thought they needed. After all, deception in service to the user is not a vice!

31

Colorful Language *

As the modern Zen master put it, what is the color of one hand clapping? Something to ponder as we take a look at color in user interfaces.

Color has become an important aspect of graphical user interfaces, at least in the selling of software. For years I resisted getting a color monitor because most of my work was straight text processing. My venerable Hercules-compatible video card gave me everything I needed, and I could work for hours in front of that flat-screen amber monochrome monitor without headaches or blurred vision. Why should I switch to anemic color, lower resolution, and the flickering jaggies? I did own a color monitor, an overgrown CGA turkey that came bundled with my first laptop, but it mostly functioned as an end table. I didn't see the software world in full color until I finally moved up to my current workhorse system, which came with 1024 by 768 video in 256 colors on a 72-hertz noninterlaced display. My eyes were opened.

Until then, I saw color as a sales gimmick for video games and executive decision support software, which are often indistinguishable. Although I never went through the usual crazies with the Windows desktop color scheme ("Look, Maude, it's psychedelic!"), I did start reassessing the role of color in communication. Color can be more than just more fun. It can be an important part of the communication between software and user. The trick, of course, is in knowing when and how to use it.

---

* From *Software Development*, Volume 1, #1, January 1993.

Colors carry certain connotations, mostly culturally shaped, but some of which may be wired in. Children, even infants, seem to show more interest in bright colors and vivid contrasts. Red, orange, and yellow, especially in an otherwise black-and-white context, draw our attention. But people do not always behave in ways consistent with conventional assumptions about color. Popular wisdom has it that blue and green are cool colors that calm the viewer, but research doesn't support this. Some studies have suggested that surroundings painted in a kind of hot pink may actually be the most psychologically and physiologically calming, even though most people hate such a decor.

Some corporate GUI standards specify that potentially risky or irreversible actions be flagged in red. Unfortunately, typical users behave in a way that defeats the intent. Rubrication actually increases the likelihood of casually selecting an item or icon. For many people, a red item in a menu is like a red flag to a bull; once they spot it, they simply have to click on it.

Color Communication

Color can be used as an added dimension of communication that can aid in interpreting complex information. Both my daughters went through an experimental public school that used an innovative approach to reading. If English were a phonetically regular language with uniform spelling, there would be little need for spell-checkers and hardly a word of debate about teaching phonics versus reading by rote. But the same sound in English can be spelled dozens of ways. In fact, many of the greatest irregularities in spelling and grammar tend to fall in the core vocabulary that has come down most directly from Proto-indo-european, which makes it harder on the young protoreader.

The Gatagno "words-in-color" system cleverly used color as an auxiliary clue to "decoding" the sounds of words. All the different forms of the "ay" sound — "eigh," "ei," "ai," "ey," "a," etc. — were printed in the same color, a sort of visual training wheels that the kids were intended to outgrow.

This clever scheme seemed to work, but it is also possible to be monumentally stupid about educational uses of color. One object-oriented methodology maven has been preaching multi-sensory educational techniques to reach the whole brain through sound and color and action. Of course, his visuals at one major conference, though projected on a magnificent high-resolution true-color display system, were just heaps of straight text in mind-numbing monochrome. The only appeal to the right brain or to that artistic seven-year-old lurking within every systems analyst was some black-and-white clip art in the lower right corner of each slide. Alas, it was the same art on each slide and had nothing to do with illustrating or reinforcing the point.

Children and other human-type creatures do learn concepts more easily and more thoroughly when communication is reinforced through representations in various media and modalities, especially when abstractions can be given colorful tangible forms that can be manipulated. Kids are helped in learning the alphabet by colored letters they can pick up and play with. Smart trainers have been using this for years. Part of the success of so-called CRC cards in object-oriented design (Wirfs-Brock et al. 1990) is that these little 3-by-5 or 4-by-6 stand-ins for object classes are concrete things that can be played with by developers as they think through various architectures and scenarios.

Our earnest methodologist, on the other hand, used colored game pieces to involve the audience in learning his pet methodology. Unfortunately, the colors, muted pastels of almost uniform saturation, were neither easily distinguishable nor very informative. The one possible pedagogical justification for the colors was overlooked altogether because tokens representing closely related concepts were given distinct rather than similar or related colors, while tokens for very different concepts were given shades of light blue-green and green-blue so similar that in the slightly dimmed light of the auditorium they were virtually indistinguishable to most people and blurred into grayish uniformity to an important minority. About one in every twelve males is color blind, along with about one out of 200 females.

Which leads to an important rule of color in user interface design: never rely on color alone to make any potentially important distinction among visual elements. If it is important to tell a static class relationship from a dynamic instance relationship, for example, then displaying one in red and the other in blue is not enough. The lines should differ in weight (thickness) or style (solid, dashed, etc.) as well.

If color is employed as an essential part of the user interface, the humble designer ought to leave open the possibility of the end user knowing best — or at least having the final say. Under Windows you can change the color of most anything, but I have never been able to figure out how to change the color of the text cursor in Windows apps. The anorexic little cursor that inhabits most text applications is almost invisible when it's the same color as the text. I ended up making the text color dark blue, which is nearly as good against a paper-white background, but makes it much easier to find that blinking cursor.

Color Scheming

As hi-res color displays begin to dominate not only the office but the lecture and conference circuit, graphics have gained new prominence, with misguided attempts by corporate sponsors of conferences to impose a standard "look-and-feel" for entire conferences through distributing "templates" for presentation packages like Persuasion or PowerPoint.

Part of the problem is that the templates are either developed by software types who have no sense of aesthetics and understand little or nothing about communicating information, or else by graphics arts types who may have a sense of aesthetics, but still know little or nothing about communicating information. The former produce the same garish garbage as can be found in many personalized desktop color schemes; the latter produce those lovely templates with lushly shaded backgrounds that have become the hallmark of the audio-visual upper class. The typical color scheme shades from rich purple through bright blue, with royal-blue headlines and mint-green "bullets." Beautiful look and feel! Only trouble is, half the audience can't read half the slides. At one recent conference nearly everyone over forty admitted to me that they couldn't read the gorgeous rear-projection displays, but instead relied on the printed handouts, which were done in black-and-white, of course.

Your corporate look-and-feelers, worried about looking and feeling good, are on the wrong track. The perception of shape depends on contrast. As a rule, greater contrast enhances readability. It has long been known that, under normal lighting conditions, text is most readable when it is presented as black text on white background. Light on dark is substantially harder to read, and color on color can be eyestrain city.

Which raises another issue: fonts. You can sometimes tell the age of the software development staff by the fonts appearing in the user interface. All too often, software uses or defaults to what I term "under-40" fonts: small print in typefaces with low line weight. Only those under 40 can read them! The problems are worsened by high-resolution displays because system fonts are usually bit-mapped. More than once I have seen a great software demo ruined because nobody gathered around the exhibit booth could actually read the menus or diagrams; they just nodded politely as if they knew what was happening.

The rising hegemony of "presentation packages" creates other problems as well. They promote what I call "six-shooter slides" — you know, bullet, bullet, bullet, bullet, bullet, bullet. Visual aids should be just that, aids to understanding and recall, visually illustrating, expanding, or reinforcing a presenter's commentary. Six-shooter visuals are the weakest and least effective way to use a potentially powerful tool. The fact that they are in pretty colors adds nothing. Color and graphics capabilities ought to be employed to some practical end in communication, not merely used willy-nilly following the Sir Edmond Hillary Principle of Design — because they are there.

Like Siskel and Ebert, I am convinced that some features are best appreciated in the original, uncolorized form. Colorful language may be best rendered in stark black-and-white. As to the color of one hand clapping, I think it may be the same color as a window.

32

Improving Intermediates[*]

Ski trails come in three varieties — green, blue, and black — because skiers, too, are of three kinds: novices, intermediates, and experts. I happen to be an intermediate skier, have been for years, and expect to be all my life. I'm what ski instructors refer to euphemistically as a classic "improving intermediate," meaning I'm middle-aged, keep getting better, but not by much and not very quickly. I'm happy. I love skiing and have even survived a few of those dreaded (or lauded) double black diamond trails, usually because I miss the last turnoff onto the kinder, gentler slopes. Mostly, though, I keep my eyes out for those user-friendly blue squares and reassuring green circles.

Skiing has a lot to teach us about the relationship between users and systems and how software developers can improve that relationship. It would be a punishing experience to learn to ski on one of those steep expert slopes strewn with bone-jarring bumps. A few tyros, mostly youngsters under twelve, seem to go directly to the mogul fields following their first try on the bunny slope, but I've always suspected that they were really bionic mutants. For most of us, those wide gentle slopes marked with friendly green circles are essential for early learning.

On the other hand, you can only learn so much if you stay all day on the bunny slopes. Sooner or later you have to move on to the bigger challenges of the blue and the black (or, occasionally, the black and blue).

---

[*] From *Software Development*, Volume 1, #2, February 1993.

The power users of skiing, experts who twist their way down the slalom course and fly over the mogul fields, would have us believe that theirs is the only way. But improving intermediates can enjoy transcendent moments, too, as when you come off the top at Heavenly Valley, with the turquoise jewel of Lake Tahoe shining below and the desert to the east, a brown and ocher sea stretching to the horizon, and the crisp morning air stings your face as you whisper through a dusting of fresh powder.

Three-phase Design

Okay, so what has this got to do with software development? Aside from day-dreaming about skiing Tahoe again, I wanted to introduce the triphasic model of human interfaces (Constantine 1994a, 1994c). The triphasic model says that system users have different needs at different stages in their development as users, and that the user interface should be designed to accommodate these changing needs. To do this, software must present different faces to users of different levels of ability, each designed with its own distinct features and particular technical goals. Like the network of trails at a good ski resort, these interface components are not really separate but are intricately interconnected.

The three interfaces in the triphasic model are the acquisition interface, the transition interface, and the production interface. The acquisition interface is the system the naïve user sees on first encounter with the software. A good acquisition interface enables the beginner to do work right from the get-go. The production interface makes it possible for an experienced, fully trained user to produce sophisticated results with high efficiency. In between is the transition interface, for the improving intermediates among software users — those who are beyond the slow and sloppy point-and-click of the beginner, but are not and may never be real power users who can slalom their way with shortcut keys through multiple applications in cascaded windows. Just as the novice, intermediate, and expert trails at the ski resort are distinct but interconnected, so a well-designed system presents a threefold interface with smooth transitions among its parts.

Disenfranchised Majority

I think one of the most serious problems in user interface design today is that most of the attention is given to laying out the bunny slopes of software. Expert users are grudgingly accommodated by leaving open access to rather rough and ugly "advanced" features or by cobbling together a random set of keystroke shortcuts and an awkward macro facility. But the "improving intermediates," who may well be the most numerous and most important category, are virtually ignored.

If a system is useful and reasonably well designed, users will not remain novices forever. A minority of them may eventually become experts or power users, but the majority will probably spend their days as improving intermediates. Their needs are neither those of experts nor novices; they need a user interface that allows them to steadily and incrementally add knowledge of the software and increase their skill in using it. It should not punish them for what they don't know or need, and it should not send them unexpectedly hurtling down the double-black-diamond slopes of dialogues only a C++ programmer could love.

At best, commercial software and software development tools seem to have green trails and double black diamonds, but almost nothing in between. The transition interface, which helps the former novice continue to improve in efficiency and versatility, needs to be designed as a distinct collection of interface features that are systematically tied to what the beginner already knows and what the expert will need to know. User-configurable button bars and tool palettes are probably a good idea but not the answer, since they either saddle users with the standard set — invariably either too complex or too limited — or make them figure out for themselves which features are which.

The entire interface could be modal, offering a novice mode and a series of intermediate modes with expanding interface richness and versatility. Novices should probably not see or be offered access to the black diamond features, except through clearly marked "lifts" or "trails." A check on a preference list tells the system what general level the user has reached or wants to use. Custom interface layouts could start from this range of standard ones. Oddly, many freeware computer games are readily configurable by player ability, but expensive productivity packages and software development tools come in one-size-fits-all configurations.

Maps

Ski resorts typically provide other user-friendly features that ought to be part of every software interface. Trail maps show how to get from where you are to where you want to be and guide the skier who is seeking out or trying to avoid certain kinds of trails. Software systems should incorporate or provide their own trail maps, visual guides to the layout of features in the maze of buttons and dialogues, pull-down and pop-up menus. On-line help, at least as typically done with the help engines of popular GUIs, is of only limited value. Such on-line un-help is every bit as difficult or clumsy to navigate as the menus and dialogues themselves and, worse, is invariably organized differently than the interface itself.

On the ski slopes, the trails themselves are clearly marked, the same way as on the map. In software, menu titles frequently give little or no clue to what lies below, and the "help" system, separated from the interface features it is supposed to help with, often employs a different vocabulary. If I am trying to figure out how to make a footnote go away in my word processor, the darned help system should just show me, opening the right menus in sequence and pointing to what I need to use.

Different tools and approaches, even different rules and principles, may apply to the transition interface than to the acquisition or production interfaces. Usability testing (see Chapter 30), which studies users actually interacting with a system, may help fine-tune the acquisition interface, but it is likely to help little with the transition or production interfaces. Why? Because the camcorder runs out of tape or the psychologist runs out of attention span long before users progress to intermediate or expert levels of ability.

With the help of good engineering and extensive usability testing, some GUIs have succeeded in furnishing a reasonable acquisition interface. The original Apple Macintosh interface was designed to a target of twenty minutes from sealed box to productive work, for example.

The problem is that, as the user progresses, the typical interface remains the same. Beginning users of a system really need what amounts to software training wheels. Training wheels have helped many a kid learn to ride a bicycle, but training wheels were not meant to be permanent. Training wheels, in fact, do not actually help kids learn to ride a bicycle; they help kids learn to ride a bicycle-with-training-wheels! In order to develop the balance and motor skills to ride a bicycle, the training wheels have to come off.

There you have it. Just when you were reluctantly ready to accept the need to design and test the user interface for your next product, you find out one interface is not enough. You need green, blue, and black versions, with trail maps and markings, and maybe even detachable training wheels. Okay, so the analogy isn't perfect.

I think I'll go and hit the slopes!

33

Unusable You[*]

2.70! The number may not be familiar, but the M.I.T. mechanical engineering course it designates is famous. Students get a kit of miscellaneous parts, then compete to design and build the best robot ping-pong ball sweeper or computerized mobile bridge or some other challenge dreamed up by faculty. Professor Woody Flowers, PBS science maven and originator of course 2.70, wants to help tomorrow's designers and engineers make more usable products that really work for humans. His undergraduate design courses have spawned competitions for high school students, and he even arms middle-school students with cameras to search out and document unfriendly or unusable designs around them.

If dumb design is so obvious, why is it that millions of VCRs and microwave ovens around the world flash 12:00 or 88:88? Why doesn't GUI-based software speed up our work? Despite human factors departments and usability testing labs, leading vendors keep on releasing stupid software with major usability problems that a 12-year-old can spot from across the room.

Consider this: My computer tells me I have 8,283 files filling nearly 550 megabytes of disk space. Making sense of and finding things in such a digital jungle is a big part of staying ahead in consulting. File size and creation date are often clues to getting the right version or variation, so we like to see these when we go to open a file from an application. A good time for basic housekeeping — rearranging files and directories, renaming or deleting material —

---

[*] From *Software Development*, Volume 2, #4, April 1994.

is while we're looking at and thinking about files as we open or save them. Everybody knows this, but only a minority of software is built this way. We need an add-on/add-in that standardizes and extends the garden variety Open, Save, and SaveAs dialogues under Windows so that every app displays file stats and descriptions and allows routine file maintenance from within the dialogue.

Good idea. Some major products supply this capability. With one such marvel installed, you hit Ctrl-O and, in the upper left of the file open dialogue, where it always was, appears the familiar combo box for file name with scrollable file list below showing, as always, too few of the files and no file stats. Highlight a file name, and a gray box in the lower right(!) reveals date, time, and size for that one file. Only one set of stats is visible at a time, visual attention must shift repeatedly between upper left and lower right, two distinct and widely separated visual elements must be mentally connected into one conceptual entity, file descriptions cannot be compared without memorizing, and instead of a quick and easy visual scan through a list, a clumsy sequential, mechanical operation is required. This brain-dead design violates basic interface design principles and fails to support the work the user is trying to accomplish.

We are not talking about rocket science; these problems are obvious to untrained teenagers. All the leading development companies have trained user interface specialists and elaborate usability testing facilities. I know from talking with these companies that they are concerned about usability issues and seem knowledgeable about user interface design principles. But something goes wrong between the intentions and the software that ships. I've been looking into some of the reasons that good companies keep shipping crummy software. A systematic investigation is in the works, but here are some of the things that stand out at this stage.

Job Description

In order to have usable software, the user interface has to be somebody's job. Without responsibility and accountability, better user interfaces don't happen. I've been saying this for years. Now I'm beginning to think that usability has to be *everyone's* job, that everyone on the development team has to be focused on end-product usability and take it seriously from first brainstorm to final box.

One way to develop this focus is through systematic usability inspections (Constantine 1994b). These resemble traditional design and code walkthroughs, but focus on the user interface and usability issues to identify usability defects. This gets developers thinking about users and issues of software usability. A single inspection just before freezing a final release is not enough. Developers and interface specialists should inspect work flow models, early paper prototypes, initial designs, and working prototypes, as well as alpha and beta versions of the software. With each successive inspection, usability improves, as Jacob Nielsen has shown (Nielsen 1993). With each inspection, developers also learn a little more about good user interface design and the defects to avoid.

Too Little, Too Late

Software developers often throw away useful findings on product usability because they get them too late. Leading vendors of development tools and other shrink-wrapped software like to prove their commitment to usability by pointing to shiny new testing labs where representative end users can be observed and evaluated with elaborate video and computer equipment as they try out software. Empirical usability testing is more glamorous than usability inspection, but lab testing has some major disadvantages. For one thing, usability testing comes too late. Realistic evaluation of end-user interaction with software requires a working system, usually a beta test version. By this time the user interface mistakes have all been made. Finding them all will be difficult to impossible. Since the basic structure and functionality of the software is cast in concrete code, it's typically too late to do more than tweak and fine-tune superficial aspects of the user interface. The result is a user interface that may be polished but is still misshapen. The real problems are often in the architecture of the software and user interface, in how the features fit together as a whole or fall apart, in the basic model on which the software is built.

Even when there are fundamental flaws in the architecture or the need for major rethinking of how the software and the user interact, usability testing often does not reveal them. It is better at identifying smaller problems within a given overall approach. Just as you can't test your way to bug-free code, you can't test your way to defect-free user interfaces.

Even expert evaluations, which are typically cheaper and more efficient than usability testing, are often conducted too late to be very useful. In one application, a thorough user interface inspection identified a little over a hundred usability defects, which were prioritized by the severity of their impact on product usability. The client fixed a handful of surface defects among the lower third of problems but only one of the dozen defects categorized as serious. The rest were all judged to be too hard to change because of the underlying program architecture.

Surface Features

Much software development is feature-driven. In the marketplace, the one who finishes with the most or the fanciest features wins. Yet feature-laden software with attractive 3-D graphics can still be seriously deficient in user interface design. Software usability resides in the total organization of the user interface, not in how features look so much as in how features work and how they work together to make the user's job easier. Getting this right takes attention to interface architecture and attention to interface detail by everyone throughout product development.

Perhaps this is why software vendors attend so much to layout, look, and feel, not because these are so important for usability, but because these are the only things they know how to fix.

34

Objects in Your Face [*]

Graphical user interfaces have nothing to do with usability, they have to do with graphics. After all, what's the point of having a fancy GUI if you don't use it to draw pretty pictures? And, with display performance a vanishing issue, why not animate your pretty pictures? The aim is marketing and the target is reviewers and software purchasers who look, but not too carefully, then write a rave review or order a site license. Users who care more about getting real work done are another group altogether, which is one reason you hear a lot more about user interfaces than usability, more about "user-centric" design philosophy than about supporting work, more about listening to the voice of the customer than about listening to the problems of workers.

Enter object technology. Where once everything had to be "structured" to be worthy of attention, now it must be "object-oriented." If it ain't object-oriented, it ain't up to date. If software is not built out of "objects" and "classes," then it can't possibly be any good. Objects, so the simplistic claims go, are natural and intuitive. What's more, they're politically correct — they're reusable!

Now user interfaces have become object-oriented. Or so it says on the outside of the box.

---

[*] Revised from *Object Magazine*, July 1993.

On the Face of It

Just when you thought you could rest in the knowledge that objects were securely ensconced where they belong: in class libraries of immense reusability and deep within the coded heart of robust software everywhere, just when you thought you finally understood polymorphism and genericity and persistent objects, just when object technology starts to make sense, suddenly, objects start appearing on your monitor screen. If objects are good inside the software, they must be good outside as well. If objects are good for developers, they must be good for users. Or so the advertising says.

So what does the object revolution look like when it escapes the programming language and reaches the user interface? Picture this: On the screen is a simulation of a pocket organizer, a "day-timer." Click on the "index tabs" to go to any section, click on the corner of a "page" and the page flips. My, how clever! Of course, most of the time half the screen is wasteland and you have to twist your neck to read the index tabs, first clockwise, then the other way, as text flips from side to side with the turning pages. Ah, but it looks familiar, and everyone knows that familiar metaphors make software easier to use, right? It is especially important not to notice that there is less information on the super-VGA screen than on an old 80-column DOS display, even though it is displayed now in a much smaller font. After all, it's in color, which is great if you are not among the one in twelve males who are color blind. This "personal information manager" must be good, because it is surrounded by and covered up by and interlaced with all those pretty pictures. But wait, they're not just pictures, they're objects! You can manipulate them and communicate with them and make your life wonderful with them.

Yet another personal information manager shows a picture of a rotary index file (such as a Rolodex™) on the screen. Click on the lid and it opens up to reveal little index cards with names, addresses, and phone numbers on them. Click and drag on the "knobs" on either side and the index cards flip past on the screen.

Some call this object-oriented, but other, more impolite names and descriptions can be heard among people who actually use this stuff. Not that we don't need extra flourishes of the mouse to add to the risk of repetitive motion injuries, not that we don't need that extra bit of a break from work while we ooh and ah over the cartoon cards flipping over in the middle of the screen. After all, this is an object-oriented user interface!

What is an object-oriented interface? Is it just icons, button bars, and pull-down menus, your garden variety icky-sticky GUI? Or is it point-and-click and drag-and-drop, the dogma of direct manipulation? (To be acronymically correct, we are now talking about OOI GUI WIMPs.) Maybe it's any user interface implemented in an object-oriented programming language, or perhaps just the user interface of any system written using OOP techniques, independent of the language. Perhaps it means the interface is peppered with pictures of "real-world" objects. Maybe users interact with the system by sending messages to objects. ("Document, print thyself.")

In truth, "object-oriented interface" simply means the object-oriented revolution is over. The new paradigm for thinking has succeeded so well that even marketing executives and ad copywriters have discovered objects. Objects sell!

Of course, we all know objects are better. They're better because objects are intuitive, and pictures are intuitive, and pictures are objects — or some such reasoning. But a quick look at the unlabeled icons on some popular new e-mail packages or word processors or presentation software will show just how intuitive these interfaces are. How many of those icons can be interpreted correctly at first glance? How many can be remembered from session to session? How many can be learned in less than a year of daily use? Whatever it says on the outside of the box the software came in, if it takes more than a second to figure out an icon, it ain't intuitive! If you forget which blob to click on to set columns, it ain't intuitive. If you keep selecting the wrong menu to make page headers, it ain't intuitive.

Does any of this matter? What difference can the shape of an icon make or the details of copy-by-click-and-drag? A lot. Small errors and small irritations add up, slowing down rather than speeding up work. Work is what some of us try to accomplish in our hours at the desk. Software that runs counter to the way people think about or carry out tasks means a permanent increase in errors. If the program makes the user do an extra step or think twice or reinterpret things, no matter how familiar it becomes, the user will continue to make more mistakes than the necessary minimum. These extra errors are, in truth, not human error at all, but defects in the interface, in the software.

The user interface *is* the system to the user; it is what end users see and interact with in trying to get work done. They do not see the clever use of multiple inheritance or the inspired construction of some method or the meticulous reuse of library classes. They do not see most of the stuff that software developers futz over so much. They see the user interface. Period. The user interface is more than just look-and-feel; it is how the system works, how it behaves. For users, the really important question about the interface of any piece of software is whether and how it lets them use the system to support their work.

Do clever icons and cute animations, dialogues in pictures, and buttons that talk make software any easier to use to accomplish real work? Work is behavior. It is made up of actions, steps and activities interconnected by other activities. It does not consist of objects but of operations. When it comes to accomplishing work, far more important than the objects are the objectives: what work is done, how work is done, and why work is done. When this is kept in mind by developers, better systems are possible, systems that help users work better.

Physical Fallacy

Back in the dark ages of the industry, when software engineering was still data processing, analysts and programmers learned the hard way that simply automating the old manual procedures led to bad systems, clumsy emulations instead of clever enhancements. Today we have "object-oriented" interfaces, and what has happened to the old Rolodex™? It has moved from the top of your desk to your so-called desktop! The implementers of these mindless models of manual systems miss the fact that the original Rolodex™ was itself a technological breakthrough, substantially departing from the clumsier technology of loose index cards, which, in turn, were a significant advancement over bound ledger books. A Rolodex™ or DayTimer™ or DayRunner™ that can be empowering when you can hold it in your hand becomes merely awkward and annoying when it is simulated on the screen.

The problem is that object technology is handicapped by some naïve mythology. Object technology guru Ivar Jacobson has noted that naïve object models lead to software that is not robust in the face of changing requirements and varied uses. Naïve object models are based on simplistically searching the application environment for "real-world" entities, then loading all behavior onto object classes based on these entities. The practice of attaching all behavior to buttons and icons based on real-world entities is equally naïve and leads to less robust interfaces.

Sound software architectures include many components, whether object classes or functional modules, that arise from the needs of the software, that are part of the solution more than part of the problem. These essential components must be created, not just discovered lying about the room in some silly "object game." Developing good internal architecture — or good interface architecture — requires the software engineer as a thinking problem solver, not as a playful painter of representational reality. Instead of naïvely allocating actions to simple stand-ins for physical pieces, good design distributes behavior and responsibilities in software components based on sound software engineering principles that keep related behavior together and leave objects uncoupled from each other.

Everyone who understands object technology knows that software objects are not real-world objects and do not behave the same. The **Patient** object in a hospital information system may legitimately be expected to know its diagnosis and the status of payment from its **Insurer**, but we do not expect it to respond to a "kneetap" message by jerking some software "leg." Objects, despite what the gaily clad gurus of object naïveté might tell you, are not "real," they are abstractions — abstractions in the minds of analysts, designers, and programmers — no more a part of the "natural" world than any of the other abstractions we humans invent to make it through the workday.

There is a real connection between object technology and good user interface design, but it is subtle and somewhat indirect. In better supporting encapsulation and information hiding, objects enable more rational and effective partitionings of the total problem into subproblems. Sound object-oriented software architecture makes it easier to keep the implementation of the user interface and the implementation of the underlying functionality of an application distinct but interrelated. Sound object-oriented software engineering subdivides object classes representing and supporting different facets of the problem (Jacobson et al. 1992). Interface objects, which encapsulate interactive behaviors with the characteristics and features of external interfaces, can be kept distinct from domain objects that encapsulate data and behavior associated with the concepts and constructs of the application domain, and from control objects that encompass coordination and communication spanning multiple objects.

To the extent that objects are an enabling technology for more effective and extensive reuse, object orientation can contribute to better user interfaces because consistent reuse builds consistent user interfaces. Consistent user interfaces are more usable because there are fewer distinct things users have to learn and remember to make effective use of them. Consistency allows users to reuse skills and procedures learned for one purpose on other parts of an interface or on other systems. Setting local text attributes from a tool bar, for example, should not be significantly different from setting text attributes as the global defaults for an entire document. However desirable it may be, consistency can be hard to achieve when every feature and facet of a user interface is separately conceived and constructed. It is substantially easier to build consistent user interfaces from standardized class libraries and project repositories of reusable object classes.

Today's short-lived "wisdom" in human–computer interaction is that good user interfaces consist of explorable collections of familiar objects. Far more important than free-form explorability is that the user interface be well organized in ways that support real work. It has to reflect the conceptual and intrinsic organization of the work, not the physical artifacts of its current incarnation. This means thinking about what users are really trying to do and what will make it easier. It means keeping simple things simple. Locating the telephone number of a colleague should not involve repeated rotations of a simulated on-screen knob. Correcting a mistake should not trigger an on-screen conflagration as a simulated wastebasket bursts into flame.

Good object interfaces are simply good user interfaces, interfaces that support work and leave people in charge. They take over things that computers do better and let humans continue to do what humans are good at. Software engineers can do better than copy the simple-minded simulacrums of today's crummy software. A typewriter is not merely a mechanical pencil. An honest-to-goodness personal information manager is not a pocket appointment book displayed on a VGA screen.

The question now for software developers and user interface designers is whether object-oriented software will be more a matter of object interfaces or objects in your face!

Brave New Software

Introduction

You cannot not communicate. This is sometimes known as the First Law of Human Communication (Watzlawick et al. 1967). All action or inaction is a form of communication — it makes a statement — and all communication is, in some sense, in some sphere, political. From pointless prattle to significant silence, communication has an impact. Language and communication are matters of syntax, semantics, and pragmatics. It's the pragmatics of human communication that makes it unavoidably political.

Software is a form of communication. As Ed Yourdon and I said way back in the turbulent 1970s, good software is written to be read; it's a message from one programmer to another programmer — or to a future self. It is also a message from the programmer to the user, filtered through the slow and somewhat inept interpreter known as the user interface, saying something to the user about how the developer viewed and made sense of the world. The system and its user interface are the media through which the programmer's mental model is communicated to the end user. Whether the message gets through and in what form depends on many things, among which both the intent and the ability of the developer are paramount.

As communication, then, software makes a political statement and plays a political role. How software portrays people, what it permits or prohibits, where it directs or misdirects the attention — these are political messages. Because it is so ubiquitous, software may well be among the most pervasive of modern day political forces. Video games that glorify violence and bloodshed, for example, are not neutral technology, but powerful messages about what the world is about. Whether you like them or abhor them, build them or would ban them, video games that make males the heroes and females the victims are playing sexual politics.

Software developers are paid to build better systems, not build a better world, or so some would claim. Science and technology seem to offer safe haven for professionals who just want to get on with the work or have fun playing with the technology. But we are not just professionals; we are also people sharing a shrinking planet. There are no balconies for a disinterested audience, only this one vast stage, the world.

What are programs for, anyway? Who do they serve? I will try not to get too preachy on you, but there are things we ought to think about as we plan and program our brave new software. What does a product say to the public, to its users? What does it communicate to those who enter into its dialogs? Does it empower people or delimit them, ennoble or demean them? Does it enlighten or does it confuse? Does it challenge and elevate or only reflect indifference? Does it make a difference?

So many questions. Your answers will determine your final grade.

Interfaces Diversified*

Diversity is not merely Politically Correct; it pays. It pays in teams, where it can contribute to a creative synergy, and in the marketplace, where diversity has become yet another fuzzword for flacks and field reps to use in their pitches. Now PC products are also P.C. products, and diversity has come to the user interface.

At one conference on CHI (Computer Human Interaction) in Boston, a presenter argued for customizing user interface design to appeal to diverse ethnic groups and user communities. The solution? Different user interface designs for different "demographics." The point was made by starting with a garden-variety dialog box for setting text attributes: font, size, style, and the like. Uninspired and utilitarian design, one might say: not optimal, but not terribly bad either. Then the diversified alternatives were displayed.

Circular Reasoning

Following the elegant understatement of a so-called "European" design (may-

* From *Software Development*, Volume 2, #8, August 1994.

be the font was Eurostile?) came the one for women: a circular dialog box with little round buttons and text arranged in arcs. Many women said it looked like a carrying case for birth-control pills. Or a compact. How appropriate!

It is irrelevant whether, as the designer argued, women are really more attracted to curvilinear shapes than are men. A text style dialog box is a tool. The real issue here is that the circular dialog would simply be substantially harder for anyone, female or male, to use. Text wrapped around a curve or tilted is much more difficult to read than regular horizontal text, and circular scrolling is simply screwy.

This design had been criticized, as the presenter acknowledged, ever since it first appeared in an ACM publication a year earlier. As a counterpoint, he briefly flashed on the screen a fairly conventional looking dialog box puta-tively designed by some female staffers. But moments later, as if to argue for the basic validity of the concept of cultural customization, a dialog box tai-lored for African-Americans was proudly displayed, with buttons and boxes awash amidst assorted shapes in saturated colors. To justify this motif, the fol-lowing slide showed the African art work on which the layout had been based. The aesthetic appeal of the African folk art is not the issue. User preferences and usability testing aside, the text boxes and buttons in this design were almost completely lost against the colorful backdrop.

This reminds me of an attempt some years ago to introduce a line of power tools for women. The company reasoned that handywoman wannabes would go for lighter tools with smaller grips. The fact that the tools were molded in "designer colors" couldn't hurt. Unfortunately, they were also under-powered and none too sturdy. Any woman really interested in doing something herself went for the real stuff: black, ugly, and useful.

Hoosiers and Africans

The kind of accommodation to diverse users exemplified by color-splashed di-alog boxes and pretty pink power tools is neither respectful nor empowering. Instead of validating and valuing genuine differences, it perpetuates silly and superficial stereotypes. It lumps real diversity under artificial and largely meaningless rubrics, creating what writer Kurt Vonnegut called a "granfal-loon," a false grouping.

After all, just who is this archetypal European who prefers left-justified labels and art deco layout? Is it an Italian or a German? What aesthetics and sensibilities do the residents of Sicily share with those of Stockholm? As the ad for the newspaper says, "The European — you can't be one without it." Only in the minds of advertising executives and corporate think-tankers is there a "European culture," as opposed to provincial French or Tuscan or Danish middle class.

We make granfalloons of many things, but especially Africa, an entire continent with dozens of distinct and very different nations, yet often treated in the media as if it were a single country and Africans a single people. Under this all-subsuming head, the interesting and important differences are lost. One ad in a recent Sunday supplement even touted a cruise to "exotic ports like Rio de Janeiro, Singapore, and Africa." Indeed. The port of Africa must have one humongous harbor!

Customization to varied tastes can be done well, without stereotyping users or sacrificing usability. For example, in a competitive playoff of designs for a computer-based voicemail interface, the team from Claris showed a main dialog with user-selectable "faceplates" that changed the overall shape and appearance without altering the basic functionality or ease of use. On the other end of the playoff panel, and at the other extreme in approaches to users, was one of the biggest software vendors, exhibiting a one-size-fits-all, plain-vanilla WIMP design. Ho, hum.

Good design takes into account the real needs and characteristics of users. Consider the lowly bicycle seat. Modern touring bikes are equipped with seats that, although seldom described as comfortable by anyone with an intact nervous system, are better suited for male posterior anatomy than female. A group of women, engineers and bike enthusiasts all, have come up with an entirely new seat design fitted to the shape of female cyclists. It's black, it's homely, but it's a lot more comfortable — or so I am told.

The bottom line for software user interfaces is to make it easy for the user to make whatever custom accommodations to taste and work habits make sense to them, changes that will enhance rather than interfere with accomplishing whatever they want to do with software.

Aesthetic Apprehension

Aesthetics are an important element of user interface design but should not hinder usability. I may customize the contents and position of a tool bar, but I don't want lace edges around messages. There is, I believe, a kind of beauty in simple practicality. Shaker furniture. Snap-On socket sets. Tools that work well, that truly fit the function and the hand of the user, are beautiful in themselves. We don't have to agree on all these matters as long as the aesthetics of software is under user control.

I spend a lot of my day facing a monitor. To me, the "wallpaper" on my desktop becomes a virtual window, like the cherished kitchen window over the sink that allows you to watch the garden while you wash the dishes. Sometimes my desktop window reveals a panorama of the cascades and cataracts of Waterfall City, as realized by artist James Gurney. Or it may look out on the robust but graceful arcs of Ron Walotsky's bridges and viaducts criss-crossing an imagined city. Sometimes the golden hues of an alien sun silhouette the elegant aerial arches of Jim Burns's Aristoi. Is this interface feminine? Typically male? American? European? Intellectual? Sensual? Who knows. You won't find it in any user interface guidebook. Although the styles of these artists, masters of modern fantastic realism, are all very different, there is a common aesthetic link: me. I'm the one who pulled these bitmaps together, so that I can gaze out over far vistas as I think about the next column.

If you want to sell your interface to more people, don't stereotype and don't put your design dogma between the user and the software. Give users something that lets them customize what matters to them, whether it's how the software looks or how it works. Then get out of the way.

Wizard Widgets[*]

An axiom of science fiction is that any sufficiently advanced technology looks like magic to the uninitiated. Even to those on the inside, who know that it's all just floating point adds and conditional logic, computers can seem a little like black magic. Some software developers would make them seem even more magical by putting wizards and agents and active intelligence on your screen.

Like a cocktail-lounge mentalist, a software wizard asks leading questions, then jumps to conclusions. A wizard in a presentation package might ask what kind of talk you are going to be making, what the main subject and secondary themes are, who will be in the audience, and what you want to accomplish. Then the wizard picks a color scheme and a slide template, then lays out your title slide for you. Maybe it's a good choice, maybe it isn't, but at least it saves you from having to think. And as long as you don't mind having visuals that look like everyone else's corporate issue, you don't need to have good taste or know anything about layout and design.

Just Acting

Steven Weiss, software methodologist and magician, once told me, "A magician is an actor playing the part of a magician." A wizard, then, must be dumb software playing the part of an intelligent actor. Even though we all know that

---

[*] From *Software Development*, Volume 2, #9, September 1994.

real magic isn't real, for some reason we're prepared to believe that artificial intelligence is real when its a simulacrum on the screen.

Even experts can be credulous about on-screen pseudo-expertise in software that simulates intelligence. I once evaluated a CASE tool that included a complex expert system to automate the conversion of an analysis model, the data flow diagram, into a design model, the module structure chart. At the time, it had been through beta testing and extensive in-house use on real projects. Not one user had ever noticed that no matter how the rules were weighted or the criteria prioritized, the system always produced the same design, a trivial mechanical transformation of the input not an intelligent design, not even a very good design. The expertise of this "intelligent" software was never questioned; its recommendations had been accepted without thought or critical evaluation.

At least wizards wait to be asked to perform their magic and otherwise stay out of the way. Not so with active agents. These next-generation TSRs sit there and watch what's going on, offering help or advice or messages from time to time. In one brave new GUI, each agent is represented by a caricature: an older woman with her gray hair in a bun is meant to be the librarian, a stern male is a resource manager, and a strange character with hat down over his eyes is supposed to be a search agent. When agents have something to say, their expression changes. They frown slightly to indicate a possible error or raise a finger and seem about to speak if they have a suggestion or message. Aside from being sexist and cast in culture-bound stereotypes, is this a good idea?

Some software vendors think that even e-mail should be active, doing things unbidden on the recipient's computer, such as launching an application or deleting itself if it lies unread. Sounds like a virus to me. I don't know about the rest of the corporate world, but I don't want my e-mail to do anything on my machine except sit there quietly until I decide what to do with it.

People anthropomorphize everything from cars to cats. Many computer users give personal names to their machines and a surprising number, including no few software developers, attribute personality to software and hardware. For some programmers this may be just a cute way of talking, but for many people it is really animism, a form of magical thinking that attributes agency and personality to nonliving and nonintelligent things. It's what we do when we don't understand or can't figure something out. We're all guilty.

My first microcomputer was, appropriately, an Exidy Sorcerer. Even with its limited RAM and low-res graphics, it could do some pretty impressive things, not all of them by design. After a full day of use it would start to drop random bits from here and there in memory. I knew the real story was that some of the RAM was marginal under thermal stress, but it sure *seemed* like the thing was getting cranky and uncooperative, like an overtired child.

If it were not for my skeptical nature and my M.I.T. background, I would even have believed the Sorcerer had a grudge against a friend of mine who would occasionally borrow it to write papers. It would be working perfectly for me, but five minutes after she sat down and started typing it would start spitting garbage onto the screen or wander off into la–la land, locked up in some remote routine or another. When I tried it again, all would be fine. I know there was a rational explanation, though we never found it, but it was hard not to believe that she and the Sorcerer just didn't get along.

Dumb Terminals

Computers do not think, of course. Even the best so-called machine intelligence is nothing more than human intelligence behind a scrim of pixels and megabytes. None of the current crop of "smart" widgets has an AIQ (Artificial Intelligence Quotient) above zero. The intelligence, if it can be whimsically called that, is faked. One usability cabalist talking about "seductive interfaces" at a recent conference said it was even possible to "simulate real intimacy" with intelligent user interfaces. It's not hard to do, he assured the audience, "You know, just like you do with your wife." His wife, maybe.

It is possible that we've already come to accept mechanical and manufactured "intimacy" as real. Letters and birthday cards and advertisements are "personalized" by machine. Most of us have received one of those photocopied advertisements with a yellow sticky-note slapped on at a casual angle: "Larry, thought you'd find this interesting, J." Everyone knows someone whose name starts with J, so we're supposed to assume this is a personal recommendation from a friend or acquaintance, when it's really just another mass-produced promotion.

Windows wizardry is a form of misdirection. Misdirection is one of the fundamental operating principles of magic, the real kind, which is to say the fake kind. If magicians point to something or wave something or talk about something, it's because they don't want you to notice something else. One of the first rules for figuring out how a trick is done is never to look where you're supposed to look. By putting faces on toolbars and creating dialog boxes that simulate intimacy, we misdirect users away from questions of what the software really ought to be doing for the them. We offer them mediocrity while calling it magic. We offer them the illusion of intelligent software, seducing them into surrendering the task of thinking to the machine. Of course, the machine isn't thinking, which means that nobody is.

Maybe software should carry warning labels likes the ones required on foodstuffs and other consumer products. "This software contains routines that pretend to be smart." Or, "Use of wizards and agents and other forms of artificial intelligence is no substitute for using your head." One modest but telling bit of research found that the more users were told about the actual logic and construction methods used in an expert system, the less likely they were to trust the software blindly. Maybe there is hope.

Future Faces[*]

What color is your PC? Does your laptop make a fashion statement? My road horse is a dark, boring gray, and my office machine is the usual grayish-tan color sometimes called "putty" by office furniture stores. But there is hope. A new line of multimedia PCs with built-in radio, television, and VCR — true "information appliances" — will come in various bright fashion colors. Might they clash with our other household appliances, which are mostly bone white or black anodized aluminum? Don't ask.

Long ago and far away, some slide rules came with a leather carrying case that clipped to a belt, but nobody actually wore them. That was then, what next? Wearable computers and computers as fashion accessories. That, according to the keynote speaker at a conference on computer–human interfaces, is what the bright minds that gave the world the computer for the rest of us are now fantasizing.

Soft Seduction

Everything old is new again. Remember those treacly "user-friendly" interfaces that greeted you by name and told you to have a nice day even though you made a boo-boo and entered an improper date? A few of the GUI gurus who didn't get the point are now going one better, proposing "seductive interfaces," interfaces for mass markets that present the computer as friend, as pal, as partner. But do

---

[*] From *Software Development*, Volume 2, #10, October 1994.

you want your computer to be a pal, or would you rather it just helped get things done?

These fantasized interfaces do not depend on any elusive artificial intelligence, at least not the authentic article pursued by computer scientists. Seductive interfaces are a marketing ploy to make software irresistible. The friendship is feigned and the seduction is simulated by customizing the interface to the personality of the customer. One audacious designer claims the programming is straightforward, since there only four different personalities anyway and everything you need to know about a person can be gleaned from about twenty questions. The last time I looked, there were at least twenty *theories* of personality and most all of them were more complex than this.

Judging from the research reports coming out of some of our major software vendors, there may be as much interest in simplified pseudo-psychology as in learning how to make software that really helps people. People want this seductive stuff, we are told. They would rather be talked to in just the right way than be able to do more. They would rather have the software take their hand and take over. But do you really want to be seduced by a computer, especially one that fakes it?

Still wilder interface dreams await: the knowledge cape, for example, a combination opera cape and truly flexible computer all rolled into one. Simply pick the cape preloaded for the occasion — advanced object-oriented software engineering for the office, current events and repartee for a party, a database of consumer reviews for that rare venture into a shopping mall. The cape would whisper in your ear to make you an expert at whatever you wanted. It could even remind you of the name of someone you ought to know, presumably keeping track of who is there in front of you through its own optics and audio input, or perhaps through some sort of neural interface yet to be devised. (It's just details; don't bother dreamers with details.) With the knowledge cape we go from computers that fake intelligence or intimacy to computers that help people fake it. What a brave new world where charm and conversational facility will devolve on whomever can afford the most RAM or the latest downloads for their knowledge capes. But do you really want to find yourself drawn to someone whose understanding comes from floppy circuitry with a velveteen lining?

Wrist Architectures

But wait, there's more, as they say in those late-night television ads. Today's cyberpunk fashion already sports tie tacks and earrings made from surplus chips and digital widgets, but tomorrow, we are told, we will be wearing the real thing. We will have complete computers in fashionable bracelets. (For those times when a cape might seem like over-dressing, I suppose.) And the wizards of interface design are even proposing that wrist computers use infrared or short-range radio to link automatically whenever they came in close proximity — using the proper protocol and digital signature verification to establish routing and the right recipient, of course. (I suppose the miniaturized versions would be called cuff links.) When friends met and shook hands, their computers could automatically exchange messages for them, giving new meaning to the phrase "handshaking protocol." What progress! Technology in service to humanity, eliminating the need for unpleasant human activity, like casual conversation or the more dread intimacy of a tête-à-tête. Wouldn't you rather swap files with a friend than talk?

The vision expands. As technology improved, the links might be varied from close range to general broadcast. You would not actually have to listen to the boor who insists on telling everyone at a party the same stupid story of how he was once stuck in an elevator with John Scully. The account would just be downloaded to your wrist processor when you entered the room. Then your own clever software, programmed to recognize the same old stuff even when it was shoveled remotely, would promptly delete it. No need to listen or even to drag-and-drop that garbage anymore.

The same wrist wonder could couple with the resident hardware when you checked into a hotel, downloading your profile to the room, adjusting the temperature and lights to your taste, and setting the wall-sized screen to the right screen-saver wallpaper. Or it might begin presenting you with personally relevant excerpts from the *Wall Street Journal* or *Software Development* or alt.wierd, as suited your tastes. In fact, one of the more common fantasies for the coming microcomputer millennium is software to search out and screen out information from the enormous digital deluge washing over the information interstates.

I already have access to such a system. My partner scans publications ranging from the *Journal* to *DBMS* and unerringly informs me about things I find interesting, enlightening, and useful. I do the same for her in other publications. Trying to put such services into computer software raises two nearly insurmountable issues. Most of the stuff that comes under the nominal headings in which I am interested is not worth reading, and many of the most valuable items fall into novel categories I could never specify in advance. Can a computer understand you well enough to fulfill this function? Would you trust it knowing that the "understanding" was faked?

Control Return

Knowledge capes or computer bracelets, word processors that rewrite your prose or software that figures out who you are — perhaps so much of this is so far in the future that we can rest easy in the knowledge that, like predicting the halting of a Turing machine, some problems are intractable in theory or in practice even if they are easy to describe. If the giant software houses can't build a presentation package without memory leaks or an operating system that doesn't flush itself into blank-screen oblivion, do we need to worry whether they'll be able to do a credible job creating software intelligence or programmed intimacy?

Alas, in the meantime the GUI designers, like fashion designers, often seem more interested in cosmetics than capabilities. Flexible interfaces adjust to the user by customization of the inconsequential. You can choose almost any color scheme you want, but don't expect accommodation to real needs and differences in working styles.

As usability guru Ben Shneiderman reminds us, people want to be in control, but they also want a sense of accomplishment. They want to be able to control real things. At the end of the day they don't want to think about all the things their software did, but about what *they* achieved. It's up to us as developers to decide what we want to accomplish. Do we want software that makes a fashion statement or that makes a difference, user interfaces that give control to the user or ones that just do a good job of faking it?

References

Ancona, D. G. and D. F. Caldwell. 1992. "Bridging the Boundary: External Activity and Performance in Organizational Teams," *Administrative Science Quarterly* 37(4): 634–65.

Anderson, L. E. and W. K. Balzer. 1991. "Effects of Timing of Leaders' Opinions on Problem-Solving Groups," *Group & Organizational Studies* 16(1): 86–101.

Belbin, R. M. 1981. *Management Teams: Why They Succeed or Fail*. London: Heinemann.

Bollinger, T. B. and C. McGowan. 1991. "A Critical Look at Software Capability Evaluations," *IEE Software* 8(4): 25–41.

Case, J. 1990. The Open-Book Managers," *Inc.* 12(9): 104–13.

Cobb, R. H. and H. D. Mills. 1990. "Engineering Software Under Statistical Quality Control," *IEEE Software* 7(6): 44–54.

Constantine, L. L. 1986. *Family Paradigms*. New York: Guilford Press.

_____. 1989. "Teamwork Paradigms and the Structured Open Team." *Proceedings: Embedded Systems Conference*. San Francisco: Miller Freeman.

_____. 1990. "Organization Paradigms and the Management of Change," *Proceedings: Software Development '90*. San Francisco: Miller Freeman.

_____. 1991a. "Building Structured Open Teams to Work," *Software Development '91 Proceedings*. San Francisco: Miller Freeman.

_____. 1991b. "Toward Usable Interfaces: Bringing Users and User Perspectives into Design," *American Programmer* 4(2): 6–14.

_____ . 1991c. "Fitting Intervention to Organization Paradigm," *Organization Development Journal* 9(2): 41–50.

_____ . 1992a. "Managing for Quality User Interfaces," *Software Management 1992 Proceedings*. San Francisco: Miller Freeman.

_____ . 1992b. "Getting the User Interface Right: Basic Principles," *Software Development 1992 Proceedings*. San Francisco: Miller Freeman.

_____ . 1992c. "Quality by Increments: Small Steps with Big Payoffs," *American Programmer* 5 (2).

_____ . 1993a. "Objects in Your Face," *Object Magazine*, July.

_____ . 1993b. "User Interface Design for Embedded Systems," *Embedded Systems Programming*, August.

_____ . 1993c. "Work Organization Paradigms for Project Management and Organizations," *Communications of the ACM* 36(10). October.

_____ . 1994a. More than Just a Pretty Face: Designing for Usability," *Software Development 1994 Proceedings*. San Francisco: Miller Freeman.

_____ . 1994b. "Collaborative Usability Inspections for Embedded Systems," *Embedded Systems Conference Proceedings*. San Francisco: Miller Freeman.

_____ . 1994c. "Interfaces for Intermediates," *IEEE Software* 11(4): 96–99.

_____ . 1994d. "Graphical Navigation," *Windows Tech Journal*, August.

DeMarco, T. 1982. *Controlling Software Projects*. New York: Yourdon Press.

DeMarco, T. and T. Lister. 1987. *Peopleware: Productive Projects and Teams*. New York: Dorset House.

Doyle, M. and M. Strauss. 1982. *How to Make Meetings Work*. New York: Jove.

Finegan, J. 1990. "The Education of Harry Featherstone," *Inc*. 12 (7): 57–66.

Fisher, R. and W. Ury. 1981. *Getting to Yes*. New York: Houghton Mifflin.

Fisher, R. and Brown. 1988. *Getting Together: Building Relationships As We Negotiate*. New York: Penguin.

Holtzblatt, K. and H. Beyer. 1993. "Making Customer-Centered Design Work for Teams," *Communications of the ACM* 36(10), October.

Humphrey, W. S., T. S. Snyder, and R. R. Willis. 1991. "Software Process Improvement at Hughes Aircraft," *IEEE Software* 8(4): 11–23.

Hyman, R. B. 1993. "Creative Chaos in High-Performance Teams: An Experience Report," *Communications of the ACM* 36(1). October.

Jacobson, I., M. Christerson, P. Jonsson, and G. Övergaard. *Object-Oriented Software Engineering: A Use Case Driven Approach*. Reading, Mass.: Addison-Wesley.

Kantor, D. K. and W. Lehr. 1975. *Inside the Family: Toward a Theory of Family Process*. San Francisco: Jossey-Bass.

Larson, C. E. and F. M. J. LaFasto. 1989. *TeamWork*. Beverly Hills: Sage.

Lickert, R. 1989. *New Patterns in Management*. New York: McGraw-Hill.

Mackenzie, D. D. 1966. "The Philosophy of Conventions," in *Concepts in Program Design*, L. L. Constantine, ed. Cambridge, Mass.: Information & Systems Press.

Newmann, P. G. 1976. "Peopleware in Systems," in *Peopleware in Systems* 15–18. Cleveland, Ohio: Association for Systems Management.

Nielsen, J. 1993. *Usability Engineering*. Boston: Academic Press.

Norman, D. O. 1988. *The Psychology of Everyday Things*. New York: Basic Books.

Page-Jones, M. 1980. *Practical Guide to Structured Systems Design*. New York: Yourdon Press.

Page-Jones, M., L. L. Constantine, and S. J. Weiss. 1990. "Modeling Object-Oriented Systems: A Uniform Object Notation," *Computer Language* 7(1), October.

Plauger, P. J. 1993. *Programming on Purpose II: Essays on Software People*. Englewood Cliffs, N.J.: Prentice Hall.

Priem, R. L. and K. H. Price. 1991. "Process and Outcome Expectations for Dialectical Inquiry, Devil's Advocacy, and Consensus Techniques of Strategic Decision Making," *Group & Organizational Studies* 16(2): 206–25.

Rettig, M. 1990. "The Practical Programmer: Software Teams," *Communications of the ACM* 33(10), October.

Thomsett, R. 1990. "Effective Project Teams: A Dilemma, A Model, A Solution," *American Programmer* 3(7/8): 25–35.

Ward, P. 1992. "The Evolution of Structured Analysis. Part II: Maturity and Its Problems," *American Programmer* 5(4): 18–29.

Watzlawick, P., J. H. Beavin, and D. D. Jackson. 1967. *Pragmatics of Human Communication*. New York: Norton.

Weinberg, G. M. and E. L. Schulman. 1974. "Goals and Performance in Computer Programming," *Human Factors* 16(1): 70–77.

Whitchurch, G. G. and L. L. Constantine. 1992. "Systems Theory," in *Sourcebook of Family Theories and Methods: A Contextual Approach*, P. B. Boss et al., eds. New York: Plenum.

Wirfs-Brock, R., B. Wilkerson, and L. Weiner. 1990. *Designing Object-Oriented Software*. Englewood Cliffs, N.J.: Prentice Hall.

Wood, J. and D. Silver. 1989. *Joint Application Design*. New York: John Wiley & Sons.

Zahniser, R. A. 1990. "Building Software in Groups," *American Programmer* 3(7/8): 50–56.

_____ . 1993. "Design by Walking Around," *Communications of the ACM* 36(10), October.

Index